Studies in
environmental
pollution

The geography
of pollution
A study of Greater Manchester

The geography of pollution
A study of Greater Manchester

C.M. Wood
N. Lee
J.A. Luker
P.J.W. Saunders
Pollution Research Unit, University of Manchester

Manchester University Press

914.272

© 1974 Manchester University Press

Published by Manchester University Press
316–324 Oxford Road, Manchester M13 9NR

ISBN 0 7190 0564 7

Made and printed in Great Britain by
William Clowes & Sons, Limited, London, Beccles and Colchester

Contents

List of figures

List of tables

Preface

The study described in this book commenced as part of a review of environmental pollution research requirements for the Science and Social Science Research Councils and was completed with financial support from the Lancashire County Council. At an early stage in the Pollution Research Unit's work it became apparent that the different types of pollution are not independent but that all are parts of a process originating in the generation of waste. It was found that this process could be most effectively studied in relation to particular geographical areas. Greater Manchester is an especially interesting choice as an area for study. It is densely populated (over 2,700,000 people in an area of about 500 square miles), heavily industrialised and, by national standards, badly polluted. In 1974 the administration of the area will be reorganised to become the Greater Manchester Metropolitan County.

While there have been some other reviews of different types of urban pollution, none have examined their geographical coincidence or endeavoured to analyse their spatial relationships with the other components of the pollution process. This book consequently describes a unique study which is relevant not only to Greater Manchester but to the general understanding of the geography of pollution and its control in the UK and elsewhere.

The book commences by discussing the spatial nature of the pollution problem and its analysis before describing the basic physical, socio-economic and industrial characteristics of Greater Manchester. The next four chapters in turn review the various kinds of air, land, water and noise pollution, the wastes from which they originate and the damage to which they give rise. The final chapter draws together the preceding work by comparing the variation in overall pollution levels between the various parts of the conurbation, and by comparing pollution in Greater Manchester with that in the North West region and in the country as a whole. It concludes by examining the policy issues (including town planning policies) of wider significance to be drawn from the study, especially those relating to disadvantaged areas. The use of specialist terminology has been avoided as far as possible and factual information has generally been presented in tables and figures. The formal model of the pollution process and the statistical analysis of its constituent relationships in Greater Manchester are set out in an Appendix.

Christopher Wood, as co-ordinator of the study, has contributed most to this book, followed by the Director of the Pollution Research Unit, Norman Lee. Alison Luker and Peter Saunders have been primarily concerned with the water pollution and damage aspects of the study. Paul Cleveland, Susan Holmes, Anne Kirkham, Cathryn Sharples, Michelle Whitworth and Josephine Wood have all contributed to the study and we have also benefited from the advice of our former colleagues, James McLoughlin and Bahador Haqjoo.

In addition, a great number of people have provided information by answering our questions at interviews and over the telephone, by replying to our letters or by completing our questionnaires. Especial mention should, however, be made of the help given by R. Bee (Manchester CB Parks Department), A. Buckley (Mersey and Weaver River Authority), B. Cunliffe (SELNEC Transportation Study Group), K. Drake (Central Electricity Generating Board), S. Hart (District Alkali Inspector), S. Mullen (Bolton CB Planning Department), J. Richards (Manchester CB Public Health Department), A. Richards (Turner Brothers Asbestos Ltd.) and P. Thursfield (Local Government Operational Research Unit) and by the Cheshire and Lancashire County Planning Departments, the Manchester Weather Centre and the North West Gas Board. In acknowledging their assistance we assume full responsibility for any errors that we may inadvertently have made and for the interpretation of the information they have provided.

C. M. Wood
N. Lee
J. A. Luker
P. J. W. Saunders
Pollution Research Unit, University of Manchester, June 1973

1 Pollution: a spatial problem

The pollution process

There is no generally accepted definition of pollution, but most contain the concepts embodied in the following: 'Pollution is the introduction by man of waste matter or surplus energy into the environment, directly or indirectly causing damage to persons other than himself, his household or those with whom he has a direct contractual relationship.'

Pollution thus originates from the generation of waste matter or surplus energy by human activity. These wastes may be gaseous or particulate emissions, aqueous effluents, solid wastes or surplus energy in the form of radiation, heat, vibration or noise. During their transmission through air or water or on land they are usually diluted but may sometimes be biologically concentrated. They may also be transformed chemically by interaction with the natural environment or with other wastes. Only if the resulting substances cause damage to animate and inanimate objects ('receptors') are they classed as environmental pollutants. 'Pollution damage' embraces direct or indirect effects on man and his environment whether to human health, materials, agriculture, wild life or to amenity. The distinctions between 'waste' and 'pollution' and between damage resulting from human and from natural sources (e.g. air-borne wastes such as sulphur dioxide from volcanoes) are thus crucial. Finally, the term pollution is restricted to situations where damage is inflicted upon people with whom the waste generator has no contractual relationship, thus excluding self-inflicted damage from, say, smoking or damage incurred during employment from, for example, coal dust.

Pollution is seen to be the end result of a process originating in the generation of waste. The various parts of this process, from the different types of waste to the resulting pollution, are represented in Figure 1. It is apparent that several methods of pollution control can be employed at different points in the pollution process. Such methods will directly influence the part of the process controlled but may also indirectly affect other parts because of repercussions elsewhere in the process. Pollution damage might be reduced, for example, by limiting waste

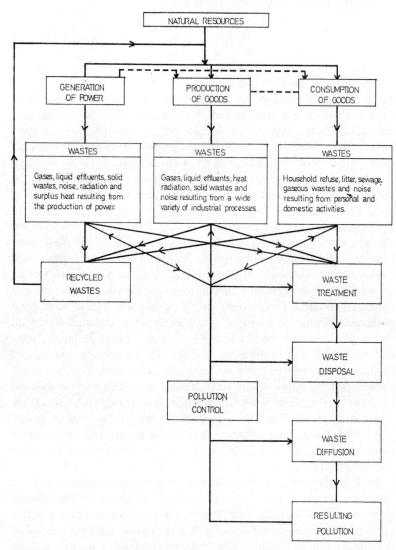

Figure 1 The pollution process

generation, by requiring more effective waste treatment, by controlling the manner and location of waste disposal, and by suitable protection and siting of sensitive receptors.

It is often convenient to classify pollutants according to the environmental medium through which they are principally diffused: air, water (freshwater and marine) and land. In many cases the environmental medium affected depends upon the manner of waste disposal. Thus a liquid chemical waste might be incinerated (leading to air pollution), diluted and run to a watercourse (freshwater pollution), or piped or dumped into the sea (marine pollution). The classification is thus somewhat arbitrary, since the environmental media are closely inter-related parts of the natural system. Noise is usually regarded as a separate category of pollution, but radioactivity, pesticides and heavy metals (depending upon their form) may be treated as types of air, water or land pollution, or as a separate group of persistent or multi-media pollutants.

Wastes are emitted into the atmosphere as either gases or particles, and are eventually removed by natural self-cleansing processes. The wastes mostly originate from the burning of fuels and the processing of materials. The pollutant concentrations to which they give rise (usually measured by the amount of pollutant per unit volume of air at ground level) are determined by the way in which the pollutant is dispersed, one of the main factors being the height at which emission takes place. Gaseous pollutants are generally quickly and uniformly dispersed through a large volume of air. The important common gaseous pollutants include oxides of sulphur, nitrogen and carbon, hydrogen sulphide, hydrogen fluoride, hydrogen chloride, hydrocarbons and ozone. By no means all these pollutants are monitored. Particulate pollutants consist of finely divided liquid or solid matter which may be small enough to remain suspended in the atmosphere for some time. The mainly solid particulates are roughly classified by size as smoke, fume, dust and grit. Their composition varies from unburnt carbon to complex substances including lead and radioactive compounds. Mists consist mostly of liquid particles.[1]

The main sources of noise are transport (road traffic and aircraft) industrial premises and domestic residences, transport noise generally being regarded as being the most significant. Noise monitoring is not yet widely practised (partly because of technical measurement difficulties) but noise levels in the environment can be estimated with reasonable accuracy if the noise properties of the sources are known.[2] Land pollution arises from the disposal of a large range of solid and liquid wastes and from the aerial deposition of trace substances including pesticides. The former include mineral, industrial and agricultural wastes, domestic refuse and sewage, pesticides and trace metals.

A wide variety of organic and inorganic substances originating as human sewage, industrial and agricultural wastes and run-off from the land, together with limited amounts emitted to the air (through aerial deposition), find their way into the river systems. The volume of water in a river, its velocity, depth and aeration affect the dilution and degredation of these effluents, and thus the water quality at any given point. The numerous water pollutants have not generally been analysed individually, water quality being determined by such measures as biochemical oxygen demand, suspended and dissolved solid content, etc. Separate analyses for metals, phenols, pesticides, nitrates, phosphates and other substances are, however, being conducted with increasing frequency.[3]

The main wastes discharged into the marine environment originate from rivers, atmospheric fallout, industrial and sewage discharges from pipe-lines and vessels and from accidental spillages (e.g. oil). With the tightening of controls over inland waste disposal during the 1960s it is suspected that a significant diversion of wastes to the marine environment has occurred.[4] The diffusion and fate of wastes in the sea is more complex than in freshwater because of tidal movements, variations in salinity and the much larger volumes of water involved. The individual pollutants are, however, similar to those found in freshwater, although they may include a wider range of toxic substances.

Despite its convenience and although most of our knowledge about pollution has tended to relate to particular environmental media, the classification of pollutants by such media has a number of limitations when the pollution process as a whole is examined. It is quite possible that wastes discharged to one medium could be substituted, at a number of different stages in the pollution process, by another set of wastes discharged to a different medium. For example, an industrial process generating airborne wastes may be superseded by another, cheaper process manufacturing a similar product but generating waterborne wastes. Similarly, changes in waste treatment may have repercussions on other media, as when incineration replaces crude domestic refuse tipping and gives rise to emissions to the atmosphere. Again, stricter controls on disposal in rivers and on land may divert wastes to the marine environment.

Once discharged, there is no guarantee that diffusion of waste will be limited to a particular environmental medium (especially in the case of persistent or cumulative substances). Thus wastes initially emitted to the atmosphere may eventually be deposited on to water or land and certain wastes, such as sulphides, discharged to the sea may enter the atmosphere. Similarly, pesticides sprayed on land may partially evaporate into the atmosphere and wastes deposited on land may run off and seep into rivers. Some persistent materials deposited in the freshwater and marine environments can be transferred through food chains to receptors and eco-systems based on land.

Spatial studies of pollution

A logical way to examine the pollution process as a whole is to study not an individual medium but all media within a given geographical area. The generation of wastes from industrial and domestic activities and their disposal, diffusion and environmental consequences within that area can then be studied comprehensively. Apart from the use of spatial studies to overcome the disadvantages of the single medium approach, such studies have considerable significance in formulating pollution policies to be administered by planning authorities, water authorities and the other control organisations. For example, a geographical area forms the natural basis for a comprehensive environmental control policy of the type discussed in Chapter 7.

The generation of wastes within an area is determined by the degree and type of land use activity to be found there. Primary, secondary and tertiary industry together with the domestic sector of the economy all contribute to the wastes arising in the area. Land use activities, and hence the wastes generated, are not uniformly distributed over the country as a whole, but vary from area to area and from one part of a particular area to another. It is therefore necessary to sub-divide any area selected for study into a number of smaller areas (zones) to take account of these variations and to permit analysis of wastes in terms of the waste generating characteristics of the zones.

The pollution to which the wastes generated give rise depends upon the diffusion characteristics of the area, i.e. upon the topography, river system, climate, etc. A given set of wastes will not create the same pollution pattern in two different areas. In the same way the damage

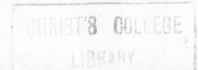

caused by the pollution depends upon the distribution and composition of receptors (population, animals, crops, parks, materials, etc.). This distribution again varies from one area to another.

The choice of the boundary and the number and size of the zones into which an area is divided is important to any spatial study, and depends upon a number of factors. There will be an exchange of wastes between areas by natural and physical transportation. The larger the area chosen, the less important this factor should be. Again, if the area consists of a single river basin or air shed (a reasonably independent body of air, as in a bowl surrounded by hills) or has a fairly self-contained economy, the pattern of exchanges will be simplified and minimised. These arguments tend to suggest the region[5] or sub-region as a study unit.

There are also transfers of pollutants between media. As mentioned earlier, heavy metals or sulphur dioxide in air may affect water quality, hydrogen sulphide in water may affect air pollution, and toxic wastes deposited on land may leach into water-courses. It is difficult to assess the importance of these exchanges, but their geographical scale appears to be large[6] and does not affect the choice between a regional or sub-regional study area to any great extent.

The study area should be sub-divided into sufficiently small zones for the distribution and characteristics of the pollution process to be examined meaningfully. However, because transfers of wastes between the zones of a sub-region occur, sub-division should not be so fine that these transfers become more important than the pollution process within a particular zone. Although theoretically a suitably sized grid square system would be desirable, the choice of local authority areas as zones is dictated by data availability. These authority areas vary considerably in size, population and level of industrial activity.

The method of analysis adopted in any comprehensive spatial study of pollution must be based upon certain simplifying assumptions. In the absence of detailed aerial and ground surveys it must be assumed, for example, that the basic determinants of waste generation (population, industrial activity, etc.) are uniformly distributed within a particular zone. For some purposes parallel assumptions about the distribution of wastes, pollution and damage must be made.

Similar assumptions are embodied in the set of equations which formally represent the various parts of the pollution process in a sub-region (see Appendix). Thus wastes discharged from each zone into the environment are related to zonal population, socio-economic, industrial and land-use characteristics. Pollution levels in each zone are described as a function of the wastes generated, with provision for the transfer of wastes across area and zonal boundaries and from one medium to another. Finally, damage is examined in terms of the pollution levels and the characteristics of receptors in each zone. All these relationships can be expressed in terms of both current and likely future situations and be developed into more realistic, though complex, forms.

Data for spatial pollution studies
The above method of analysis, even in its simplified form, demands a formidable information input. For a given zone, data on different air-borne wastes (emissions to atmosphere), water-borne wastes (effluents to rivers and run-off from land), solid wastes (domestic, trade and industrial wastes of every type) and noise (aircraft, traffic, industrial and domestic noise) are required. In order to relate these wastes to the zone from which they originate, data on population, socio-economic characteristics of the population and level and composition of industrial activity (the basic parameters) within the zone are needed. Again, knowledge of the imports and exports of wastes across zonal boundaries is necessary. The ground-level concentration of air pollution in each zone is needed, as is the 'contact' level for pollutants and receptors in the other media. In addition, it is necessary to establish some satisfactory measure of the receptor characteristics of each zone and the damage suffered by them. Finally, the analysis requires not only a considerable quantity of information but also consistency between the various information inputs. (For example, all data on wastes and their basic determinants should relate to the same time period.)

Greater Manchester data
Four main methods of obtaining information about pollution were employed in the study described in this book. The first was the use of published sources, which provided data on population and its socio-economic characteristics, industrial structure, air pollution concentrations, derelict land, etc. The second method involved the use of interviews. A large number of visits were made to officers employed in local and central government, water and other statutory undertakings, river authorities and to university and industrial staff. These interviews yielded a considerable quantity of information and the various organisations visited frequently provided access to unpublished data (e.g. on

road traffic). The third method entailed the use of questionnaires to local government officers. In all, six questionnaires were despatched to each local authority, though in many cases the same officer acted in two roles, or for more than one authority. Each questionnaire was addressed to the officer concerned by name[7] and accompanied by a letter and a circular note describing the general purposes of the study. A reminder and second questionnaire were sent to those officers not replying within a week of the completion date.

The questionnaires were despatched to Chief Public Health Inspectors, Cleansing Officers, Sewage Works Managers, Parks and Cemeteries Superintendents, Medical Officers of Health and Public Analysts and requested information relating to pollution within the officers' fields of interest. The response rates and a synopsis of the types of data obtained are shown in Table 1.

Officers	Data Requested	Response Rate	Response Percentage
Chief Public Health Inspector	Pollution generally, complaints	62/68	91
Cleansing Officer	Solid wastes, refuse, litter	63/68	90
Sewage Works Manager	Influents, effluents to water courses, sludge disposal	46/63	73
Parks & Cemeteries Superintendent	Damage to materials and plants	50/68	74
Medical Officer of Health	Damage to health	12/26	46
Public Analyst	Analyses of water, air, food	4/10	40
All		253/303	78

Table 1   Data obtained from and response to postal
questionnaires

The questionnaire returns and accompanying data (contained, for example, in copies of recent annual reports) proved to be invaluable in eliciting otherwise unavailable information about methods of refuse and sludge disposal, public complaints about pollution damage to materials and vegetation and about any local pollution surveys.

The last method of generating information was by estimation and interpolation. If data for several zones had already been obtained, this could sometimes be used to estimate values for other zones or for the whole study area. In other cases it proved possible to use pollution as a basis for calculating waste or even as an indication of waste, or vice versa, although there are of course dangers inherent in this procedure.[8] For obvious reasons these techniques were used very sparingly.

The quality of the data obtained from these sources was variable. The published information was regarded as providing basic reference material, whereas the unpublished data elicited at interviews were treated with rather more reservation. It was generally difficult to check the accuracy of the questionnaire returns but where this was possible the information was found to be reasonably compatible with that collected from other sources. The replies to questions requiring the expression of opinions were treated with considerable care. The greatest caution, however, was necessary when interpreting complaints data.

There is no general agreement between local authorities about the definition of a complaint and a representation from an organisation is weighted equally in the statistics with one from an individual. Further-more, complaints relate mainly to those spheres in which the local officers involved have power to act. Again, considerable difficulty arises in distinguishing between complaints about pollution and those about damage. Finally, in Greater Manchester, it was noticeable that the number of complaints tended to be lowest in the large authority and low income areas. For these reasons complaints data are unlikely to be reliable indicators of pollution damage.

The information collected revealed a number of deficiencies which are discussed in more detail in the succeeding chapters of this book. On the whole, information about the basic determinants of waste generation for each zone was relatively satisfactory (Chapter 2). While the air-borne emissions, solid wastes, aqueous effluents and noise generated by certain sources were reasonably well documented, information about all types of wastes from other sources was quite inadequate. Perhaps the most important data deficiency, however, relates to pollutant levels. Certain air pollutants are monitored, but there is generally little information about concentrations of particular water pollutants, about the pollution attributable to solid wastes and about noise levels. The largest gaps in knowledge concerned damage, information being limited mostly to human mortality statistics and some detailed reports of specific, very localised damage to other receptors.

The Greater Manchester study

In view of the short-fall of relevant information outlined above, it is not at present possible to complete in detail the type of spatial pollution analysis outlined in the Appendix. Nevertheless, the general features of the model outlined have been adhered to in this study and, although it has proved necessary to treat each environmental medium separately, their interconnections are recognised at a number of points.

The next chapter deals with the basic determinants of wastes in Greater Manchester and provides the necessary background for the following chapters. Chapter 3 presents information and analysis relating to air-borne wastes, air pollution, damage from air pollution and their future levels. Chapter 4 describes the generation of solid wastes and the pollution attributable to their disposal on land. Chapter 5 is concerned with aqueous effluents discharged to rivers and canals in the conurbation and the pollution to which they give rise. Noise from motor vehicle, aircraft, industrial and domestic sources is discussed in Chapter 6.

The final chapter of the book presents an overview, drawing together the main findings on all four types of pollution. The first part of the chapter deals with the variation in different types of pollution between local authorities within the conurbation and describes the calculation of a composite pollution index for each zone in the study area. The overall pollution situation in Greater Manchester is then compared with that in the North West region and in the country as a whole. Likely future trends in pollution levels in the sub-region are also discussed. The chapter concludes with an examination of the policy implications[9] that can be drawn from this study, especially for the new authorities which commence operations in 1974.

2 The Greater Manchester area

The Greater Manchester metropolitan county proposed in 1971[10] (Figure 2) is bounded to the north east, north west and south east by the Pennines or their foothills. Consequently the sub-region falls largely within a single river basin, that of the Mersey, and may be regarded for most purposes as forming a single air shed. It is composed of 71 local authorities, covers an area of about 500 square miles and has a popu-

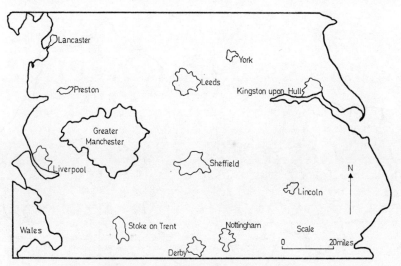

Figure 2 Greater Manchester's setting

lation of approximately $2\frac{3}{4}$ million. Greater Manchester thus fulfils many of the requirements outlined in Chapter 1 for an area suitable for a spatial study of pollution. In addition, it has a high population density and is heavily industrialised, characteristics which make it particularly interesting from a pollution standpoint.

Figure 3 shows the local authority composition of the conurbation[10] and gives the total areas of the constituent authorities. Two of the 71 local authorities which were to be included in whole or in part in the

Greater Manchester Metropolitan County (Wilmslow UD and the parish of Poynton, in Macclesfield RD) have subsequently been excluded by Parliament.[11] For the purposes of this book, however, the boundary of the county originally proposed has been retained. Some statistical adjustment has been necessary in places to take account of existing local authority areas only partially included in the new county. Throughout the book individual local authorities are referred to by both name and number for easy identification. (For example: Manchester CB (3) or Kearsley UD (44)).

Physical characteristics and climate
The principal physical features of the Greater Manchester area are

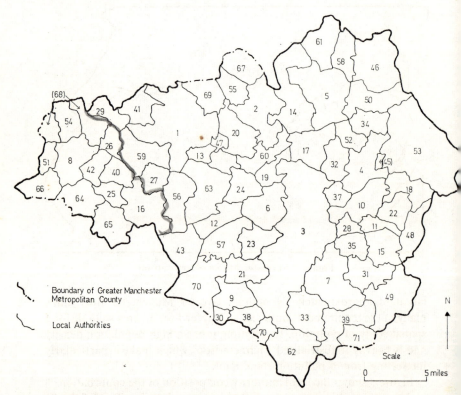

Figure 3   Local authority boundaries in Greater Manchester (see key opposite)

Local Authorities wholly included

County Boroughs	Area (acres)			Area (acres)			Area (acres)
1 Bolton	15,280	23 Stretford	3,533		42 Ince-in-Makerfield	2,321
2 Bury	7,433	24 Swinton &			43 Irlam	4,717
3 Manchester	27,255	Pendlebury	3,362		44 Kearsley	1,727
4 Oldham	6,392				45 Lees	288
5 Rochdale	9,556	Urban Districts			46 Littleborough	7,855
6 Salford	5,203				47 Little Lever	807
7 Stockport	8,440	25 Abram	1,979		48 Longdendale	3,545
8 Wigan	5,083	26 Aspull	1,905		49 Marple	7,130
		27 Atherton	2,265		50 Milnrow	5,194
Municipal Boroughs		28 Audenshaw	1,241		51 Orrell	1,616
		29 Blackrod	2,392		52 Royton	2,148
9 Altrincham	3,477	30 Bowden	1,090		53 Saddleworth	18,485
10 Ashton-u-Lyne	4,135	31 Bredbury &			54 Standish-with-	
11 Dukinfield	1,725	Romiley	4,290		Langtree	3,266
12 Eccles	3,417	32 Chadderton	3,014		55 Tottington	2,542
13 Farnworth	1,504	33 Cheadle & Gatley	5,299		56 Tyldesley	5,175
14 Heywood	8,508	34 Crompton	2,865		57 Urmston	4,799
15 Hyde	4,170	35 Denton	2,593		58 Wardle	3,192
16 Leigh	6,359	36 Droylsden	1,245		59 Westhoughton	5,560
17 Middleton	5,172	37 Failsworth	1,679		60 Whitefield	3,391
18 Mossley	3,661	38 Hale	2,264		61 Whitworth	4,483
19 Prestwich	2,421	39 Hazel Grove &			62 Wilmslow	7,691
20 Radcliffe	4,957	Bramhall	5,990		63 Worsley	7,240
21 Sale	3,629	40 Hindley	2,610			
22 Stalybridge	3,190	41 Horwich	3,257			

Local authorities of which the following parts are included

The greater part	Total Area (acres)	Approximately half	Total Area (acres)	A small part	Total Area (acres)
64 Ashton-in-Makerfield UD	6,266	66 Billinge & Winstanley UD	4,596	69 Turton UD	17,334
65 Golborne UD	7,567	67 Ramsbottom UD	9,562	70 Bucklow RD	46,103
		68 Wigan RD	11,695	71 Macclesfield RD	72,533

The estimated area of Greater Manchester is 334,000 acres (about 520 sq. miles)

shown in Figure 4. The hills bounding the area to the north and east rise to over 1400 feet above sea level and swing round to the north west, south east and, though much lower, to the south, approximating to the watershed of the Mersey river system. The upland rivers drain into the south west of the area which is less than 200 feet above sea level.

The various rivers in the area are mostly linked by the Manchester Ship Canal and the Mersey (which is partly canalised into and partly

independent of the Ship Canal) eventually emptying into the Mersey
estuary. The rivers have varying and variable flows, the modal value of
the majority being in the range 6–40 million gallons per day (mgd). The
Irwell and the Mersey above the Ship Canal have modal flows of 125

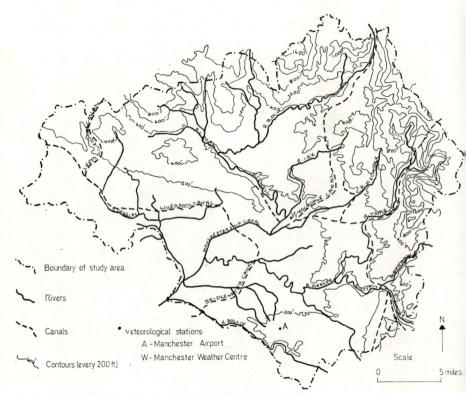

Figure 4   Relief, drainage and canal system of Greater Manchester

and 91 mgd respectively while that of the Manchester Ship Canal is
223 mgd.[12] To the west of the area a low watershed causes the upper
reaches of some rivers to drain away from the Mersey, but the volumes
involved are small. Apart from the Ship Canal, other canals form an
independent system of waterways (Figure 4).

Figure 4 also shows the two main Meteorological Office climatological
stations within the conurbation. The Airport is on the urban/rural fringe

of the sub-region, whereas the Weather Centre is situated in the middle of the central authority, Manchester CB (3). Certain measurements (e.g. rainfall) are also made at other stations. Large urban areas like Greater Manchester affect the climate in a number of ways: temperature and rainfall are increased and relative humidity, windspeed, sunshine and visibility are decreased in comparison with the surrounding rural areas.[13] The climate of Greater Manchester is affected by the Welsh mountains which, although some distance from the conurbation, provide a degree of shelter from moist south-westerly winds. As a result the sub-region has one of the drier atmospheres in the country and a low rainfall for an area close to the western seaboard. Variations in climate within the conurbation are consequently governed by mountain shelter effects as well as by degree of urbanisation, distance from the sea, altitude and topography.[14]

The two Manchester weather station sites generally have lower rainfall than the national average.[15] However, in the summer months of May, June, July and August, the Weather Centre records a higher rainfall than the average and it has more rain than the Airport throughout the year.[16] The amount of rainfall in Greater Manchester generally is closely related to altitude. The Weather Centre records slightly lower temperatures than the average for the country as a whole but higher than the North West regional average.[5] At the Airport, on the other hand, temperatures are lower than in the region as a whole and are consistently lower than at the Weather Centre.[16]

The comparative dryness of the atmosphere is the most distinctive feature of the climate of Greater Manchester. Between 1957 and 1966, for example, Ringway (altitude 76 m) had an average 2131 hours per annum with relative humidity 90% or more, whereas Heathrow Airport (altitude 25 m) had 2836 hours.[14] In general, frequencies of high relative humidity occurrences within the conurbation increase with altitude. The prevailing winds blow from the south west, the frequency of strong winds in the Greater Manchester area decreasing with distance from the coast and tending to be greater in the afternoons. Winds, which are generally stronger at the Airport than at the Weather Centre,[16] blow from every point of the compass and those from the north and east, although less frequent than the south westerlies, are generally associated with the low speeds unfavourable to the dispersion of atmospheric pollutants. There is, unfortunately, very little information available about inversions (periods of atmospheric stability when the air closest to the ground is unable to circulate and disperse the entrained pollution) over Greater Manchester.

'Fog' is defined as being associated with visibility less than 1000 m. 'Dense' fogs (visibility less than 40 m) occur only infrequently but 'thick' fogs (visibility less than 200 m) are more common. There are considerable variations in the incidence of fog from year to year. Generally, however, frequencies increase through the autumn and early winter to a January peak and then decline. During most months, the greatest fog frequencies occur within an hour or two of sunrise. Using moving averages it can be shown that the number of days on which visibility was less than 1000 m at 0900 hours at the Weather Centre [17] has decreased by about 40% between 1960 and 1970 over the year as a whole, during the winter and during the months November–January. On the other hand, the frequency of denser fogs (visibility less than 500 m) has not diminished to the same extent. The number of days on which this type of fog occurred at any time of the day or night decreased by 10% over the year as a whole, by 15% in winter and by 25% during November–January. There has also been a decrease in the frequency of fog observations at the Airport during the 1960s.[18] In general, the Airport has rather fewer fogs (i.e. visibility less than 1000 m) but rather more denser fogs (visibility less than 500 m) than the Weather Centre.[17] The number of days on which fog was observed at 0900 hours at the Airport fell by about 15% over the year as a whole, by 25% during the winter and by over 40% during November–January over the last decade.

The number of hours of sunshine tends to be lower in Greater Manchester than in England and Wales as a whole,[15] the Airport having considerably more sun than the Weather Centre.[16] In general, annual and monthly average sunshine durations decrease from west to east across the conurbation. Sunshine data for Manchester CB (3),[19] the Airport, Bolton CB (1) and Rochdale CB (5) show clearly that annual total sunshine hours in the first three locations have all increased since 1950, despite pronounced annual variations, whereas values for Rochdale CB (5) and for the England and Wales average show no discernible trend. The relationships between air pollution and sunshine and between air pollution and visibility are discussed in Chapter 3.

Population and social-economic characteristics

The populations of the various local authorities in 1951, 1961, 1966 and 1971 are shown in Table 2.[20-22] The populations of the inner core of

Local Auth- ority No.	1951	1961	1966	1971	Local Auth- ority No.	1951	1961	1966	1971
1	167,167	160,789	153,580	153,977	37	18,705	19,819	22,720	23,233
2	58,838	60,149	62,750	67,776	38	12,152	14,800	15,970	17,030
3	703,082	661,791	598,640	541,468	39	19,674	29,917	34,340	39,534
4	123,218	115,346	110,410	105,705	40	19,415	19,396	21,250	24,307
5	88,429	85,787	86,900	91,344	41	15,549	16,078	15,940	16,433
6	178,194	155,090	142,250	130,641	42	20,413	18,019	16,510	15,929
7	141,801	142,543	139,420	139,633	43	15,063	15,371	17,600	20,571
8	84,560	78,698	76,420	81,258	44	10,677	10,296	11,200	11,243
9	39,789	41,122	39,290	40,752	45	4,160	3,730	3,800	4,367
10	52,089	50,154	47,610	48,865	46	10,986	10,552	11,000	11,987
11	18,451	17,316	16,460	17,294	47	4,704	5,085	6,500	9,124
12	43,926	43,173	39,520	38,413	48	4,591	4,626	7,600	10,351
13	28,616	27,502	27,680	26,841	49	13,073	16,300	21,930	23,217
14	25,201	24,090	29,780	30,418	50	8,587	8,129	9,200	10,329
15	31,494	31,741	37,280	37,075	51	9,318	10,664	11,800	12,069
16	48,728	46,174	45,600	46,117	52	14,781	14,474	17,750	20,319
17	32,607	56,668	57,020	53,419	53	16,761	17,024	18,710	20,525
18	10,422	9,776	9,800	10,055	54	8,998	9,692	10,600	11,159
19	34,466	34,209	33,440	32,838	55	5,824	5,649	6,700	9,740
20	27,556	26,726	28,210	29,320	56	18,101	16,813	18,090	21,163
21	43,168	51,336	54,490	55,623	57	39,237	43,068	43,000	44,523
22	22,541	21,947	21,630	22,782	58	4,892	4,608	4,700	5,334
23	61,874	60,364	57,990	54,011	59	15,004	16,260	17,440	17,729
24	41,309	40,470	40,560	40,124	60	12,914	14,372	17,050	21,841
25	6,284	6,004	6,200	6,472	61	7,444	7,064	7,400	7,417
26	6,522	6,748	7,300	7,510	62	19,536	21,389	27,220	28,982
27	20,596	19,756	20,540	21,758	63	27,361	40,393	47,500	49,573
28	12,661	12,122	11,850	11,887	64	19,057	19,262	23,090	26,271
29	3,153	3,606	4,500	4,801	65	16,878	21,310	25,740	28,178
30	3,529	4,477	4,700	4,825	66	6,157	6,945	9,900	11,379
31	17,667	21,621	26,590	28,472	67	14,589	13,817	14,500	15,872
32	31,124	32,568	30,940	32,406	68	8,216	10,157	11,900	14,851
33	31,511	45,621	54,180	60,648	69	10,956	13,698	18,400	21,500
34	12,559	12,708	15,000	17,027	70	11,185	17,299	18,560	20,169
35	25,603	31,089	36,100	38,107	71	19,878	23,351	26,960	28,090
36	26,881	25,461	24,800	24,134					

Table 2 Population by local authority, 1951, 1961, 1966 and 1971

local authorities in Greater Manchester have declined sharply over the last two decades, whereas those of the outer authorities have increased markedly, especially in the south. The county boroughs in other parts of the conurbation have generally also lost population to their surrounding authorities. Overall, there has been a slight rise in population of 0·5% between 1961–71, although a modest fall was recorded for the shorter period 1966–71.

Table 3 shows the 1966 population density of each local authority,

Local Authority No.	Socio-Economic Grouping Index	Car Ownership (cars/1000)	Total Employment/Acre	Employment in SIC classes 2-18/Acre	Population/Acre	Local Authority No.	Socio-Economic Grouping Index	Car Ownership (cars/1000)	Total Employment/Acre	Employment in SIC classes 2-18/Acre	Population/Acre
1	365	126	5.3	3.1	10.1	37	354	137	3.8	2.0	13.5
2	350	151	4.4	2.7	8.4	38	288	309	1.2	0.3	7.1
3	370	101	14.2	6.1	22.0	39	291	288	2.2	1.6	5.7
4	373	106	9.7	5.7	17.3	40	385		2.4	1.3	8.3
5	357	132	4.8	3.1	9.1	41	352	147	2.3	1.7	4.9
6	382	79	13.6	6.9	27.3	42	404		2.1	1.3	7.1
7	355	145	7.7	4.0	16.5	43	371	137	2.0	1.5	3.7
8	377	107	8.1	4.0	15.0	44	359	144	1.5	1.0	6.5
9	334	182	5.8	3.3	11.3	45	350		3.8	2.5	13.0
10	364	118	5.5	2.6	11.5	46	347	127	0.7	0.5	1.4
11	368	130	3.5	2.4	9.5	47	370		3.1	2.4	8.0
12	368	122	5.7	3.2	11.6	48	346		0.5	0.3	2.2
13	368	116	8.4	4.3	18.4	49	299	262	0.6	0.3	3.1
14	377	127	1.5	0.9	3.5	50	347	166	0.8	0.6	1.8
15	366	130	5.0	3.7	8.9	51	360	125	2.2	1.5	7.3
16	382	111	4.1	2.8	7.2	52	376	146	3.5	2.7	8.3
17	363	130	3.6	2.4	11.0	53	307	214			1.0
18	379		0.9	0.5	2.6	54	370		1.0	0.8	3.2
19	330	176	2.6	0.6	13.8	55	321	175	0.5	0.2	2.6
20	358	141	3.1	2.4	5.7	56	372	140	1.6	1.1	3.5
21	315	211	3.1	1.1	15.0	57	336		4.6	2.8	9.0
22	362	120	3.3	2.5	6.8	58	348	127	0.7	0.4	1.5
23	364	122	15.1	11.3	16.4	59	327	182	0.9	0.6	3.1
24	361	144	5.9	4.2	12.1	60	326	173	1.1	0.6	5.3
25	383		0.6	0.4	3.1	61	385	114	0.6	0.4	1.7
26	388	127	0.7	0.6	4.5	62	306	277	1.0	0.3	3.5
27	388		3.6	2.2	9.1	63	358	152	2.4	1.7	6.6
28	335		4.1	2.9	9.8	64	357	145	0.9	0.5	3.7
29	366		0.3	0.1	1.9	65	341	186	1.1	0.5	3.4
30	242		0.9	0.1	4.3	66	362		0.4	0.2	2.2
31	325	183	2.6	2.0	6.2	67	345	159	0.6	0.5	1.5
32	358	150	5.1	3.9	10.3	68	341		0.3	0.2	1.1
33	297	255	2.4	1.0	10.2	69	324	219			1.1
34	375	166	2.7	2.1	5.2	70	341	231			0.4
35	341	148	4.4	3.0	13.9	71	309	297			0.4
36	350	130	5.0	2.9	19.9						

Table 3 Socio-economic grouping index, car ownership, total employment density, industrial employment density and population density by local authority, 1966

the mean number of persons per acre in Greater Manchester being 8·0 (the equivalent densities for Great Britain and England were 0·9 and 1·4). Despite their fall in population, the inner urban areas retain the highest population densities, while the north-easterly authorities close to the Pennines have the lowest. Figure 5 reveals a multinodal picture of a number of densely populated areas surrounded by authorities of lower population density.

No population forecasts for individual local authorities, apart from isolated planning estimates, have been prepared. However, estimates based upon regional sub-divisions appear to show a rise in population of rather more than 2% between 1968 and 1981 for the Greater Manchester area as a whole.[23] Similar modest increases in total population over the next decade were forecast in the South East Lancashire and

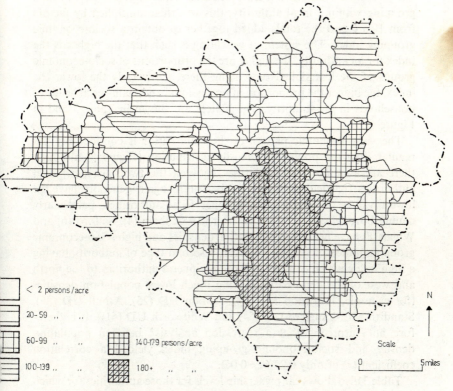

< 2 persons/acre

20-59 ,,   ,,

60-99 ,,   ,,   140-179 persons/acre

100-139 ,,   ,,   180+   ,,   ,,

N

Scale

0   5miles

Figure 5   Local authority population densities, 1966

North East Cheshire (SELNEC) Transportation Study area (which is similar to the metropolitan county except for the exclusion of Wigan CB (8) and surrounding authorities).[24] However, it has been estimated that by the later date 1991, a decline in population of $3\frac{1}{2}$–7% from the 1966 level for the whole conurbation may have occurred.[25] Within the conurbation existing trends are likely to continue, with the central areas of Bolton CB (1), Bury CB (2) and Rochdale CB (5) expected to lose more than 50% of their population to surrounding districts by 1981.[24]

The socio-economic characteristics of each local authority in 1966 (the latest date for which detailed census data have been published) were identified using the 17 socio-economic groups employed by the General Register Office[26] which were combined to create six groupings now in fairly common use. Having established the percentage of males in each grouping within a local authority, this was then multiplied by factors from 1 to 6 and the totals added together to obtain a socio-economic grouping index. The system of weighting is such that the higher is the index for an authority, the higher are the proportions of socio-economic groups of the less skilled type living there. Conversely the lower the index, the higher the proportion of professional and managerial heads of households in an authority. The indices are shown in Table 3 and in Figure 6.

The socio-economic pattern of the conurbation is considerably less regular than the population density distribution (Figure 5) although there are a number of similarities between the two. The peripheral authorities (particularly those to the south) again generally have the lowest values. Similarly, certain inner local authorities, particularly county boroughs such as Manchester (3), Oldham (4), Salford (6) and Wigan (8) have both high population densities and high socio-economic grouping indices. There is, however, a second type of authority having a high index which consists of more peripheral authorities to the north and west of the conurbation having much lower population densities (for example, Heywood MB (14), Abram UD (25), Aspull UD (26), Standish-with-Langtree UD (54) and Whitworth UD (61)). It is therefore not surprising that a regression analysis* between population density and socio-economic grouping index yielded a correlation coefficient (r) of only 0·22 $(\alpha=0·05)$.

Table 3 also shows car ownership levels for those authorities for which data could be obtained[21] and a strong association between car ownership and socio-economic grouping index can be observed. This is formally confirmed by regression analysis, the 'r' value being high (0·90) and the level of significance of the relationship between the variables being 99·95% $(\alpha=0·0005)$. It was not possible to elicit statistics for

* A statistical technique which tests the level of association between two or more variables. In this case the level of significance of the relationship was 95%; $\alpha = 0·05$. In other words, there was a 5 in 100 possibility that the r value arose because the association between the two variables was due to chance. See also the Appendix.

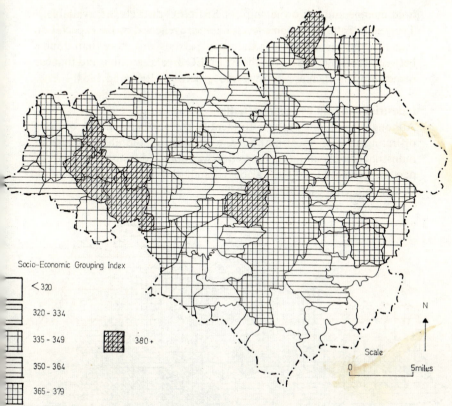

Socio-Economic Grouping Index

< 320

320 - 334

335 - 349   380 +

350 - 364

365 - 379

Figure 6   Local authority socio-economic grouping indices, 1966

household income by local authority but income and car ownership information was obtained for SELNEC districts.[27] The correlation between income and car ownership was again very significant ($r=0.88$, $\alpha=0.0005$) and both socio-economic grouping index and car ownership can therefore be used as reasonable proxies for household income. The relationship between car ownership and the population density of both local authority areas and SELNEC districts is fairly strong ($\alpha=0.0005$), and that between income and district population density is similar ($r=0.45$, $\alpha=0.0005$): the higher is the per capita income of a district, the lower its population density tends to be.

No forecasts of socio-economic characteristics of local authorities appear to have been prepared. However, 1981 forecasts of mean household income and car ownership for SELNEC districts are available.[24] The generally higher income levels likely are reflected by the expectation that the number of cars per thousand persons will more than double between 1966 and 1981 over the SELNEC area as a whole and that car ownership will increase by over 150% between 1966 and 1984.

Industrial and land use characteristics
Although it was not possible to identify the number and size of firms operating in each local authority, a measure of the absolute size of industrial activity and its composition was obtained from the number of persons employed in the various Standard Industrial Classification Orders in each local authority.[26, 28]

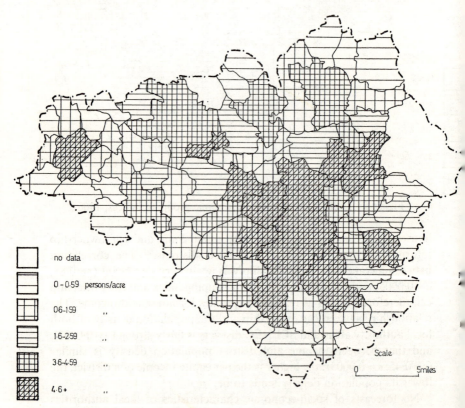

no data

0 - 0·59 persons/acre

0·6-1·59 ,,

1·6-2·59 ,,

3·6-4·59 ,,

4·6+ ,,

Scale

0 _____ 5miles

Figure 7 Local authority manufacturing employment densities, 1966

There are several difficulties involved in using employment data as indicators of industrial activity but, in the absence of information about such other measures as industrial output by local authority, they represent the best available proxy. The 1966 Greater Manchester employment statistics have been summarised in Table 3 which shows industrial employment (the 'Production Index' Orders[15] 2–18 inclusive) and total employment per acre in each local authority. Industrial employment per acre is shown in Figure 7 which illustrates the importance of the urban core areas as industrial centres, with Wigan CB (8) forming a separate smaller core. There is a pronounced decline in manufacturing employment densities towards the periphery of the conurbation closely reflecting the population density pattern in Figure 5 ($r = 0.77$, $\alpha = 0.0005$). Fairly strong correlations exist between manufacturing employment density and car ownership ($r = -0.47$, $\alpha = 0.0005$) and socio-economic grouping index ($r = 0.29$, $\alpha = 0.01$).

The main sources of employment in Greater Manchester are in distributive trades, engineering and electrical goods, textiles, professional, scientific and miscellaneous services, construction and transport. Overall the sub-regional employment pattern is not dissimilar from that of the country as a whole,[15] the most important differences being the higher proportions employed in textiles and in engineering and the lower proportions engaged in public administration and professional and scientific services in Greater Manchester. However, 55% of all employment is in manufacturing industry, compared with a national average of 50%. In addition, employment densities are much higher than in Great Britain, the total employment density in the conurbation being 4·0 persons per acre (0·4) and manufacturing employment density 2·2 (0·2).

Within the conurbation, the pattern of industrial employment varies considerably between local authorities. For example, metals manufacture is concentrated in Irlam UD (43), Manchester CB (3), Bolton CB (1), Swinton and Pendlebury MB (24) and Urmston UD (57). Textile employment is now mainly to be found in five county boroughs, Manchester (3), Rochdale (5), Bolton (1), Oldham (4) and Bury (2). Employment in the paper industry is centred in Manchester CB (3), Salford CB (6), Bury CB (2) and Radcliffe MB (20) and in chemicals in Manchester CB (3), Stretford MB (23), Urmston UD (57), Salford CB (6) and Hyde MB (15).

There have been considerable changes in the industrial structure of

Greater Manchester over the last decade. Employment declined by 9% between 1961 and 1970, compared with a growth of 1·5% in Great Britain.[29] Employment in textiles fell by 30% between 1961–8, in clothing and footwear by 20% and in coal mining by about one third. Detailed employment forecasts for Greater Manchester are not available but total employment in the SELNEC area as a whole is expected to fall by about 2% and manufacturing employment by about 8% by 1981.[24]

A number of land use maps of parts of all the Greater Manchester area are available,[30] mostly drawn up during the early 1960s. Despite a number of shortcomings, the data represented are useful in locating both emittors (e.g. livestock, industry) and receptors (e.g. crops, residential areas) of pollutants. These data indicate that much of the sub-region is devoted to urban/industrial uses, agriculture being predominant only in a number of peripheral areas although certain intensive units are to be found in the inner authorities. Some 30% of the total acreage of the conurbation is in fact devoted to agriculture, most of which (about 80%) is grassland and supports livestock, the remainder mainly being used to grow cereals, potatoes and horticultural products.[31] A further 6–7% of the total acreage is used for outdoor recreation, allotments and cemeteries.[32, 33] The only land use forecasts obtainable are from local planning authority development plans which give some indication of likely future activity patterns.

Road traffic characteristics
The main source of information on road traffic within Greater Manchester is the 1966 SELNEC Transportation Study. The 70 SELNEC districts and their relationship with local authority boundaries are shown in Figure 8. The 'district' follows local authority boundaries in that certain larger and more central authorities are divided into two or more districts whereas a number of outer authorities may be combined into a single district. In addition to data relating to car ownership, population, employment, etc., the Study obtained information about the length of major road links within each district and their traffic flow in passenger car unit equivalents (pcu's) during the peak daily period.[34]

The traffic data are derived from a traffic allocation model, rather than actual vehicle counts, and although the traffic estimates for 'corridors' are known to be reasonably accurate, this is less true for individual road links. The passenger car equivalent is a statistical unit weighting a particular mix of cars, buses and goods vehicles, one pcu mile consisting of 0·622 car miles, 0·251 goods vehicle miles and 0·004 bus miles. The average co-efficient for the conversion of peak period pcu's into 24 hour pcu's is 10·78, and it is assumed that this and the preceding average coefficients apply to each road link in the SELNEC area.

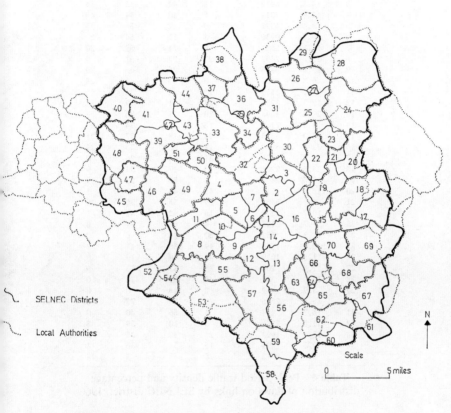

Figure 8   SELNEC district and local authority boundaries

The traffic assignments in the SELNEC study were only undertaken for through traffic (i.e. traffic travelling across zonal boundaries), it being assumed that any additional local traffic on the links would offset the through traffic which uses minor roads rather than the main roads (links). Even were this the case, the purely local traffic and through traffic using the minor roads in a district are ignored in the flow statistics

District Number	Total Link Length (miles)	pcu miles / sq.mile	% Distribution (pcu 's)			
			0-500	500-1000	1000-2000	2000+
1	19.6	17962	10	55	25	10
2	19.6	5786	17	29	37	17
3	14.2	3412	11	44	32	13
4	12.8	4314	8	10	34	48
5	9.4	5328	0	9	56	35
6	9.4	10936	3	15	54	28
7	11.6	5851	6	21	53	20
8	13.8	2497	22	27	51	0
9	19.5	6435	8	26	46	20
10	6.8	3554	0	4	68	28
11	14.1	3318	15	34	33	16
12	12.3	3235	28	41	19	12
13	28.2	4603	20	21	36	23
14	19.4	7185	15	31	34	20
15	12.0	3345	24	18	37	21
16	32.2	5720	13	27	36	24
17	15.7	1485	31	43	26	0
18	23.5	2226	40	17	34	9
19	10.5	2197	6	55	20	19
20	16.4	1711	46	44	9	1
21	8.9	5866	29	35	36	0
22	10.7	2201	16	42	41	1
23	7.7	2143	8	61	31	0
24	13.3	532	50	44	6	0
25	12.9	1886	19	38	41	2
26	11.8	1019	41	40	19	0
27	2.4	7208	33	33	33	0
28	10.0	537	45	31	24	0
29	3.9	659	62	48	0	0
30	15.5	2596	0	20	72	8
31	16.7	484	4	56	40	0
32	11.5	2278	3	10	39	48
33	18.1	1693	25	40	35	0
34	9.3	1894	15	38	36	11
35	3.6	9192	28	55	3	14

Table 4 Peak period traffic density and percentage distribution of flows on links by SELNEC district, 1966

so that the total vehicle mileage in all districts tends to be understated. Traffic loadings in the Greater Manchester area have obviously risen considerably since 1966 so the SELNEC data represent a serious underestimate of present-day traffic conditions. Increases in traffic since 1966 vary from zero in the Central Manchester district to perhaps 6% per annum, or 50% by 1973 on links in certain surrounding and outer districts.[34]

By bringing together the peak traffic flow data for the 3000 single

District Number	Total Link Length (miles)	pcu miles / sq.mile	% Distribution (pcu 's)			
			0-500	500-1000	1000-2000	2000+
36	10.8	1662	0	57	43	0
37	7.2	780	69	31	0	0
38	10.1	426	59	40	1	0
39	21.0	2659	31	32	32	5
40	7.3	743	30	60	10	0
41	20.6	863	39	53	8	0
42	3.9	7144	10	28	62	0
43	12.7	2076	56	20	24	0
44	12.1	1092	55	13	32	0
45	12.8	1769	42	35	22	1
46	12.2	2844	16	19	31	34
47	10.2	1862	44	26	30	0
48	19.2	1733	27	29	44	1
49	18.1	2758	11	16	29	44
50	3.5	2479	0	0	51	49
51	7.3	4302	19	12	55	14
52	6.9	1759	13	0	55	32
53	30.7	1713	36	38	20	6
54	10.8	847	71	21	8	0
55	12.8	3047	3	52	20	25
56	14.0	2869	7	28	58	7
57	25.4	3392	22	37	30	11
58	13.3	800	52	35	13	0
59	17.3	1031	65	20	15	0
60	7.9	949	29	44	27	0
61	9.0	1370	45	21	34	0
62	20.4	1734	33	41	20	6
63	9.8	2272	19	51	28	2
64	5.7	19526	14	50	18	18
65	17.7	2863	45	28	25	2
66	11.9	3696	4	15	57	24
67	12.1	374	88	4	8	0
68	11.1	1660	12	59	26	3
69	22.4	1433	42	36	20	2
70	6.9	2614	0	7	70	23

Table 4 (cont.)

direction road links on a district basis, it was possible to establish the proportion of each district's main road network carrying different traffic volumes. As was to be expected, the peripheral districts of the SELNEC area were shown to have considerably lower proportions of densely trafficked links than the central ones (Table 4).

The total number of peak period pcu miles travelled in each district was estimated by multiplying the peak traffic flow along each link by its length and adding the pcu mileages. The total for the district was then

divided by its area to obtain a measure of average traffic density (Table 4
and Figure 9). Central Manchester and the centres of other county
boroughs record the highest values of this measure although this may
partially result from the nature of the journey to work data used. The

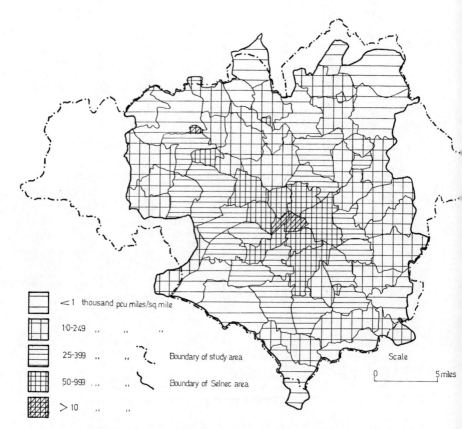

Figure 9   SELNEC district peak period traffic densities, 1966

pattern differs to some degree from that revealed by the road link traffic
statistics but the peripheral districts again record much lower values
than the central ones.

Further dispersion of resident and working populations and changes
in car ownership levels are the dominant factors underlying the forecast
80% increase in pcu trips in the SELNEC area between 1966 and 1984.

The data[34] indicate that the rate of road traffic increase is unlikely to be uniform in all districts and, since many of the additional trips will be for leisure purposes, they may not follow existing traffic patterns. It was not possible to estimate total pcu miles per square mile or the loadings on individual links by district in 1984 other than by assuming them to be proportional to trips, so that traffic volume forecasts must necessarily be very approximate. It does appear, however, that increases of 30–40% in pcu mileage are likely in some districts by 1984, whereas much larger increases of up to 180% are possible in others (especially in the present low income areas partially encircling the centre of the conurbation).

Pollution control authorities
Within the Greater Manchester sub-region there is a considerable number of different control authorities operating at different stages in the pollution process (Figure 1) and generally dealing with different pollutants.[35] Local planning authorities exert control over most types of pollution by determining whether or not a development which may result in pollution will take place. Control of a product or process, on the other hand, can decide whether or not a particular product will be manufactured and how it will be used (e.g. Department of Trade and Industry regulations on flying times and procedures to control noise from aircraft, police enforcement or motor vehicle construction and use regulations to control noise and fumes). Control over the method of treatment of waste can be employed to ensure that treatment plant of the correct specification is installed (e.g. Alkali Inspectorate control over air pollution from registered industrial processes by 'best practicable means'). Finally, control over the disposal of wastes (end-of-pipe control) can be used to fix the place, rate and method of discharge of wastes and is the most widely practised method of pollution control in this country. This is the technique employed by local authority Public Health Inspectors who control domestic and some industrial air pollution and are also responsible for certain noise problems. The River Authorities control disposal of wastes to inland water-courses and estuaries by imposing 'consent' conditions on discharges. Statutory Water Undertakers are involved in a similar way where discharges take place on gathering grounds or close to pumping stations. The Sea Fisheries Committees are concerned with discharges to marine waters other than estuaries.

There are consequently numerous authorities involved in the control

of pollution in the Greater Manchester area and their geographical
areas of jurisdiction seldom coincide, as Figure 10 shows. In all, 71 local
authorities currently exercise a control function. Much of the area falls
within the South East Lancashire and North East Cheshire Black Area,[36]
and a considerable proportion is now covered by smoke control orders
(42% of premises by the end of 1970—only 16 of the authorities in the

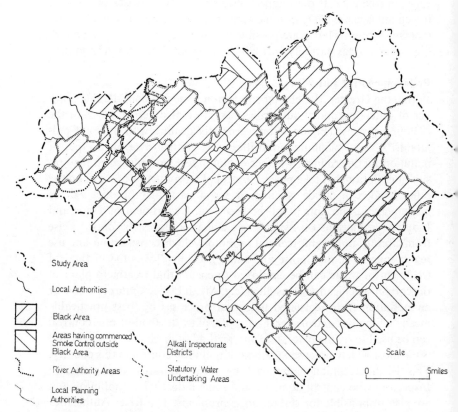

Figure 10   Pollution control authorities in Greater Manchester, 1973

whole of the conurbation having no premises currently controlled),
progress since 1966 having been marked.[36] The number of local planning
authorities is smaller, consisting of the eight county boroughs and three
county councils (although these operate delegation schemes with the
local authorities, so that many planning decisions are taken at local

level). In addition, there are two Alkali Inspectorate districts involved, district E covering the greater part of the conurbation. Similarly there are two River Authorities responsible for the area, the Mersey and Weaver administering all but a little of the conurbation and the Lancashire River Authority the remainder. There are five main Water Undertakers; the Bolton and Manchester County Borough Councils and the Makerfield, Stockport and District and West Pennine Water Boards, although others are responsible for very small areas to the west of the conurbation. The Lancashire and Western Sea Fisheries Committee has some jurisdiction over that part of the sea into which most of the conurbation's marine disposals take place.

The whole pollution control system will be radically amended by the reorganisation of local authority[11] and water authority[37] structures in April 1974 which will reduce the total number of control authorities considerably. The most appropriate administrative form of pollution control within the Greater Manchester area (and within other metropolitan areas) is therefore very much a live issue which is discussed further in Chapter 7.

3 Air pollution

The discharge of waste in the air pollution process is termed an emission. After dispersion the substances involved are measured as ground level concentrations. In other words, emissions refer to wastes and concentrations to pollution, provided they give rise to damage. This chapter deals first with emissions, then with concentrations and finally with the effects of air pollution, although there is necessarily a degree of overlap between these topics.

The first section commences by discussing wastes from the industrial processes carried on in works registered under the Alkali, etc. Works Regulation Act 1906, and is followed by an examination of emissions from road traffic. The second section considers the concentrations of pollutants from motor vehicles, the concentrations of grit and dust and of certain other pollutants and, finally, smoke and sulphur dioxide levels. The final section of the chapter describes the effects of air pollution on weather, on human health, on plants and on other receptors in Greater Manchester.

Emissions

The major contributor to atmospheric gaseous and particulate loadings is the burning of fuel to generate heat and power. Detailed statistics on the increasing consumption of gas by all users over a number of years were obtained for each local authority[38] from which time series of emissions for each authority area in Greater Manchester could be calculated by the application of coefficients.[39] The quantities of wastes emitted are, however, very small indeed. The much more significant coal and oil consumption statistics could not be obtained for the Greater Manchester area as a whole, much less for individual authorities. Even where statistics relating to the final use of fuel in the region as a whole are available,[40] the corresponding information about fuel used in energy conversion (i.e. in coke ovens, gas manufacture, etc.) is not. A detailed local survey would therefore be necessary to ascertain the consumption of these fuels and the emissions to which they give rise.

National statistics relating to emissions from various sources are available[41] which show the magnitude of domestic and industrial emissions of smoke and sulphur dioxide. Despite the absence of fuel consumption statistics from which to calculate emissions on a local authority basis it is possible to use population and employment size to calculate Greater Manchester's approximate emissions of domestic and industrial smoke and sulphur dioxide. Using national employment and population[15] and emission statistics[41] it is estimated that about 25,000 tons of sulphur dioxide and 30,000 tons of smoke are emitted annually from domestic services and that for industry the corresponding emissions are about 14,000 and 6,500 tons p.a. respectively.

These calculations assume that the national and sub-regional waste coefficients are identical. In fact these totals may be underestimates because coal consumption per head is higher in the North West than in any region other than the North and the sulphur content of the coal burned is the highest of all the regions.[42] Thus domestic smoke and sulphur dioxide emissions per head from coal in the North West are respectively the second largest and the largest amongst all the regions in the country. The domestic and industrial use of coal both nationally and in the North West region is declining rapidly,[40] so that emissions of smoke and sulphur dioxide are falling correspondingly. Oil gives rise to little smoke and only the heavy fuel oil burned in commercial and industrial boilers omits sulphur dioxide in quantities similar to the equivalent amount of coal.

As in the case of smoke and sulphur dioxide, no estimates of larger particulate matter (grit and dust) from industrial boilers or from domestic, agricultural, construction and road traffic (other than exhaust) sources could be made for Greater Manchester. One important source about which emission data on grit and dust and sulphur dioxide emissions in Greater Manchester are available is electricity generation, which is discussed below.

Registered works
There are approximately 100 works registered under the Alkali, etc. Works Regulation Act 1906 and the Alkali and Works Orders 1966 and 1971 in the Greater Manchester area.[43] These are works in which the 'best practicable means shall be used to prevent the escape of noxious gases or particulates from registered processes, whether directly or indirectly, into the atmosphere and for rendering such wastes where discharged harmless and inoffensive.'[44] The areas immediately

surrounding the works may still, however, be subject to some pollution damage from time to time. The numbers of works registered and the types of process operated in each local authority are shown in Figure 11. In all, there are about 150 users of 32 processes in the works registered in 41 local authorities, there being no such works in 30 of the Greater Manchester authorities. The concentration of the chemical industry along the Manchester Ship Canal is apparent from Figure 11, as are the attendant air and water pollution implications.

Many registered works, especially in the chemicals and metals industries, operate more than one process and many of the works registered for a single chemical substance are not chemical manufacturers but make the chemical for use in a textile or paper-making process. The environmental effects of a particular process thus vary from one works to another. For example, the pollution from the works making iron and steel in Irlam UD (43) is bound to be considerably greater than that from the works refining steel in small furnaces in Ashton-under-Lyne MB (10). Both are registered as iron and steel works. Neither the number of processes operated nor the number of registered works in a local authority is therefore a reliable indication of the level of industrial air pollution, except perhaps in the case of particulates from electricity generation and minerals processing.

Two conflicting trends are likely to affect emissions from registered works in the future. The number of works and processes registered under the current Order in Greater Manchester is falling [43] and seems likely to continue to do so. This fact, taken with the gradual tightening of controls being imposed, will tend to reduce emissions. On the other hand, the national tendency towards larger operating units means that more waste may be generated in a particular locality, tending to nullify the trend towards better control of each ton of waste created. Similarly, 'accidents' giving rise to uncontrolled emissions are likely to have more serious consequences as operations become larger. On balance, however, it seems possible that net quantities of waste generated may fall and that pollution levels will decline correspondingly in the future.

The general dearth of information about registered works does not apply to the 12 power stations in the Greater Manchester area for which sulphur dioxide and particulate emission data were obtained. [45] Due to a considerable decline in the quantity of coal and coke burnt in the sub-region (only partially offset by increases in oil consumption) the emissions of sulphur dioxide from electricity generation halved from

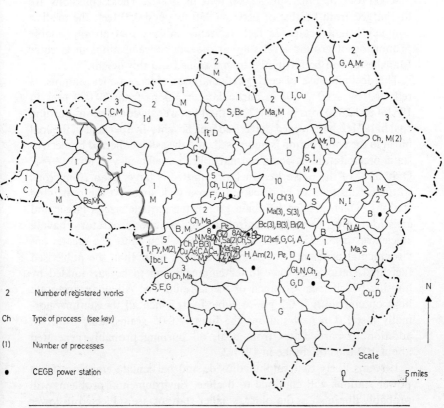

Symbol	Process	Symbol	Process	Symbol	Process	Symbol	Process
A	Ammonia	C	Ceramic	G	Gas and coke	M	Mineral
Ac	Acrylates	Ca	Cadmium	Gl	Gas liquor	Ma	Muriatic acid
Al	Aluminium	Ch	Chlorine	H	Hydrogen cyanide	Mf	Metal recovery
Am	Amines	Ci	Chemical	I	Iron and steel	N	Nitric acid
As	Acid sludge		incineration	b	Blast furnace	P	Paraffin oil
B	Bisulphite	Cu	Copper	c	Open hearth	Pe	Petroleum
Bc	Bisulphide	D	Di-isocyanates	e	Electric arc	Py	Pyridine
	of carbon	E	Electricity	f	Cupola	S	Sulphide
Br	Bromine		(not CEGB)	i	Oxygen	Sa	Sulphuric acid
Bs	Zinc	F	Fluorine	L	Lead	T	Tar

Figure 11 Local authority registered works and processes, 1973

164,000 tons in 1962/3 to 82,000 tons in 1971/2. These emissions are discharged from heights of between 230 feet and 450 feet, the median chimney height being 325 feet. It seems unlikely that an appreciable proportion of ground level sulphur dioxide concentrations in Greater Manchester can be attributed to emissions from this height.[46]

The declining use of coal, particularly at older, smaller stations, is reflected by a 60% fall in particulate emissions from 29,000 tons in 1963/4 to 12,300 tons in 1971/2. Of the 14 power station sections burning coal in 1971/2, half burned pulverised fuel. Seventy-five per cent of the coal burnt in the conurbation is pulverised, and the ash is collected by electrostatic precipitators having a normal collection efficiency of above 97%. Only 25% of the pulverised fuel ash emitted is larger than 20 microns so the wastes tend to be dispersed over a wide area. At the remaining stations, which are fed by chain grates, the particle size is larger and emissions are normally controlled by cyclone separators having efficiencies of 55–75%. It is these stations which cause the greater environmental problems since they tend to be older than the pulverised fuel fired stations, to have lower chimneys and to be surrounded by housing which receives much of the fall-out. The Alkali Inspectorate limit on emissions is 0·2 grains/cubic foot, which all the stations normally meet. (On new stations the limit is 0·05 grains/cubic foot.) In addition to particulates from coal, oil burning probably generated about 100 tons of smoke in 1971/2.

It seems likely that sulphur dioxide and particulate emissions from power stations will continue to decline. Environmental problems will probably diminish as the older, smaller stations are subjected to lower load factors when new, much larger power stations are commissioned outside the conurbation.

Road traffic

The most appropriate indicator of emissions and pollution from motor vehicles is probably traffic density (pcu miles/sq mile). Statistics for each SELNEC district were shown in Table 4 and in Figure 9. In order to convert these statistics into weights of pollutant emitted it was first necessary to convert the 'pcu miles' unit into the number of miles travelled by petrol and diesel-engined vehicles (1 pcu mile consists of 0·71 petrol plus 0·17 diesel vehicle miles), then to determine how much fuel was used by the petrol and diesel vehicles (about 23 mpg and 14 mpg respectively). The penultimate step was to establish the quantities of pollutants created per gallon of petrol and derv fuel, the factors in Table 5 summarising several reported sets of coefficients weighted towards English conditions. The final step was the combined use of emission rates, fuel usage and pcu mileage data to derive pollutant quantities per 1000 pcu miles (also shown in Table 5).

Pollutant	Petrol (1000 galls)	Diesel (1000 galls.)	1000 pcu miles (petrol & diesel)
carbon monoxide	3600	120	112
hydrocarbons	480	240	18
oxides of nitrogen	120	240	6.5
particulates	13	130	2
sulphur dioxide	10	55	1
organic acids	6	35	0.6
aldehydes	6	12	0.3
lead	4	-	0.15

Table 5 Pollutants emitted by consumption of fuels and pcu miles travelled (lbs)

Using the Table 5 coefficients and the peak period pcu data for districts and links (Table 4) it is possible to estimate the weight of different kinds of emissions produced by road traffic in each district. For illustrative purposes, the weight of wastes created per square mile in certain

Pollutant	1:Manchester Central	6:Salford East	14: Manchester South Central	58:Alderley Edge & Wilmslow South
carbon monoxide	3030	1220	800	90
hydrocarbons	490	195	130	15
oxides of nitrogen	175	70	45	5.0
particulate	55	20	14	1.5
sulphur dioxide	25	10	7.0	1.0
organic acids	16	6.5	4.5	0.5
aldehydes	8.0	3.5	2.0	0.2
lead	2.5	1.0	0.7	0.1

Table 6 Pollutants emitted in certain SELNEC districts during the peak period, 1966 (lbs/sq mile)

districts as the result of one daily peak traffic period are shown in Table 6. Central Manchester has the highest peak period traffic density in the SELNEC area, whereas Salford East and Manchester South Central are two districts having very high pcu mileage in relation to district residential population density. By way of contrast, the weights of emissions per square mile in Alderley Edge and Wilmslow are comparatively low.

Over the SELNEC area as a whole, approximately 5000 tons of carbon monoxide, 80 tons of hydrocarbons, 29 tons of oxides of nitrogen, 9 tons of particulates, 4·5 tons of sulphur dioxide, 2·7 tons of organic acids, 1·3 tons of aldehydes and 0·7 tons of lead were emitted each working day in 1966. The annual carbon monoxide emission approached 1·5 million tons. As explained in Chapter 2, these 1966 tonnages are calculated from figures relating only to traffic travelling through a particular district, taking no account of local traffic and are hence likely to considerably underestimate current emissions.

Using traffic density (pcu miles/sq mile) as an indication of the relative importance of vehicle emissions from through traffic by district, a number of correlations with different socio-economic variables were examined. The districts experiencing the largest emissions per square mile had the lowest car ownership rates (see Appendix), indicating that the traffic originating in one district is emitting much of its waste in others. Similarly, the highest emissions per square mile arise in the lowest income areas, which tend also to be the mostly densely populated. Indices of the environmental impact of emissions from both through and local traffic, based upon the traffic density and population density of a district were calculated. These indices, which indicate the relative degree to which the population is affected by wastes in different districts, show that the less affluent districts tend to experience the highest degree of environmental degradation not only from through traffic but from local traffic as well.

It is clear that the quantities of pollutants emitted in the future will depend both on traffic density and on the degree of control imposed on emissions. In Britain, controls on lead, on carbon monoxide and hydrocarbons [47] and on diesel particulates [48] are to be enforced from 1973 onwards. It is not yet clear precisely what effects these controls will have on emissions. If, however, it were to be assumed that no control over emissions takes place by 1984, then the average emission level in the conurbation might rise by 75%. The increase in the central districts having the greatest current emission densities would probably be less than this, though still of a significant order.

If, on the other hand, it is assumed that the proposed 1975 US maximum emissions standards [49] were to be imposed in this country by 1984, there would be a dramatic fall in emissions in comparison with 1966 levels (Table 7). The quantities of wastes generated per square mile in the busiest districts would nevertheless still be higher than in the lightly trafficked districts in 1966. Application of the proposed 1980 US standards would cause even more striking reductions (Table 7). It needs

Pollutant	1:Manchester Central	6: Salford East	14:Manchester South Central	58:Alderley Edge and Wilmslow South
carbon monoxide				
uncontrolled	4300	1800	1300	140
US 1975 standard	860	360	260	30
US 1980 standard	370	155	110	1
hydrocarbons				
uncontrolled	690	290	210	20
US 1975 standard	30	12	9.0	0.9
US 1980 standard	14	6.0	4.5	0.5
oxides of nitrogen				
uncontrolled	250	105	75	8.0
US 1975 standard	30	14	10	1.0
US 1980 standard	14	6.0	4.5	0.5
particulates				
uncontrolled	75	30	25	2.5
US 1975 standard	17	7.0	5.0	0.6
US 1980 standard	5.0	2.0	1.5	0.2

Table 7 Pollutants emitted in certain SELNEC districts during the peak period with varying control standards, 1984 (lbs/sq mile)

to be emphasised that both sets of standards are very much more stringent than those being enforced in the UK. Also, there is no reason to suppose that the less affluent districts will cease to bear the greatest environmental impact in the future.

Concentrations
Information about concentrations of air pollutants in Greater Manchester relates mainly to smoke, sulphur dioxide and dust and grit. However, isolated measurements of other pollutants, including some of

those emanating from motor vehicles, have been made in the conurbation.

Road traffic pollutants

There is evidence to suggest that these pollutant concentrations are directly proportional to traffic concentrations in pcu's per mile.[50] However, there is no rigorous method of translating emissions to pollutant concentrations (the determining parameters including traffic speed and wind velocity) and therefore whilst it would be possible to isolate the links carrying the most traffic, local concentrations cannot be predicted with any great confidence.

Measurements of carbon monoxide in air[51] have been made in Central Manchester using a continuous sampling device located in a busy main street. Over a 15 month period values were higher than 10 ppm for 16% of the time, higher than 30 ppm for 0·5% of the time and higher than 50 ppm (the recommended Threshold Limit value for industrial atmospheres) for 0·02% of the time. A peak value of 98 ppm was briefly recorded but carbon monoxide concentrations did not approach values normally considered deleterious to health. No significant correlation with traffic flow was found but concentrations were below 5 ppm between midnight and 7 a.m., normally reaching a peak in the morning and another, more prominent, peak during the evening rush hour.

A large scale survey of lead concentrations in dust from road gutters, pavements, parks and play areas in Greater Manchester[52] showed no significant correlation with SELNEC district traffic densities. Samples were taken from main roads, through streets, very minor streets and from sites some distance from roads. There was no significant difference in lead content between the samples from these four types of site, the average lead concentration of a total of 400 samples being 965 ppm with a standard deviation of 46 ppm and a range of 0–10,000 ppm. (These values should not be considered comparable with the concentrations of pollutants determined while air-borne.) The highest readings could be explained by local sources (paint chippings, etc.) whereas the very lowest concentrations were all obtained at least half a mile from the nearest road. Apart from the absence of low readings close to roads, concentrations were found to fall with distance from the centre of Manchester CB (3) roughly following the traffic density pattern, as in the case of lead in mosses (below). There was some evidence that levels were highest along an axis running from the city centre to the north east, the most heavily urbanised part of the conurbation.[52] Apart from these analyses at least one local authority is measuring lead in dusts[53] and all are reviewing the sources of environmental lead within their areas.[54]

Lead has been measured in mosses at least 20 metres from roads at varying distances from the centre of Manchester.[55] The results show a marked decline from about 130 ppm ($\pm$20) in the centre of the city to 90 ppm ($\pm$15) in the outer, southern suburbs and to about 70 ppm ($\pm$15) in the rural areas beyond the boundary of the Greater Manchester area. There appears to be some relationship between concentrations and traffic flows in the vicinity of measurement sites although there are other, industrial, sources of lead within the conurbation. Analyses of peat layers in upland areas indicate that, away from roads, general atmospheric lead levels may not have changed significantly over the last 100 years.[55]

Lead concentrations in the air in Manchester CB (3) have been estimated by analysing the smoke stains obtained during daily smoke measurements.[56] The average lead content at two sites was 0·7 μg/m^3 (range 0·45–1·10) in 1969. The annual average concentration for twelve provincial cities was 0·5 μg/m^3, only Stoke-on-Trent (0·9 μg/m^3) having a higher concentration than Manchester, perhaps a consequence of the ceramic industry. The average reading for London, however, was considerably higher,[56] probably reflecting its higher traffic densities.

No measurements of concentrations of motor vehicle pollutants other than carbon monoxide and lead appear to have been made in Greater Manchester. In London, however, measurements of oxides of nitrogen, hydrocarbons and the constituents of photochemical smog (for example, ozone) have been made. There appears to be no reason to suppose that the elevated levels of oxidants found there[57] on hot summer days do not occur in Greater Manchester. In other words, under certain weather conditions, the sub-region probably experiences some of the effects of mild photochemical smog.

Grit, dust and other pollutants
The monthly fall-out of grit and dust in the conurbation has been measured with deposit gauges at about 100 monitoring stations over the last decade. A procedure similar to that used for smoke and sulphur dioxide (page 44) was adopted to abstract the mean summer, winter and annual means together with the highest monthly figures for

deposited material.[58, 59] The number of sets of readings was as large as
90 in some cases, so that trends in ground level concentrations could be
calculated. There are, however, far fewer deposit gauge readings than
volumetric measurements for any one year and the calculation of means
is therefore less satisfactory. Figure 12 shows that mean winter, summer
and annual particulate values are very similar and have declined by a

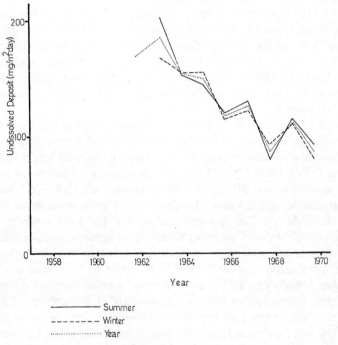

Figure 12   Greater Manchester mean grit and dust concentrations,
1961–70

factor of just under two over the last decade. Since not all the sites are in
urban areas, agricultural sources as well as industrial, domestic and
construction sources may also influence these mean values. An analysis
of national particulate matter readings (using a different approach to
take account of the many different types of area in which gauges are
located) showed little change over the country as a whole during the
last decade.[41]

There are insufficient deposit gauge readings to map the distribution of grit and dust levels. There is no clear pattern of measurements but, in general, the highest readings occur in industrial areas, as in the large Trafford Park complex in Stretford MB (23) and Urmston UD (57). If sufficient measurements were available, a pattern of peaks reflecting the locations of other 'heavy' industrial areas might be expected, with lower values indicating agricultural and other industrial sources.

It seems probable that grit and dust concentrations in the predominantly urban Greater Manchester area will in general continue to fall as power stations and other stationary sources emit less particulate material. Particulates from industrial processes (as opposed to heating or power generation) should not rise appreciably, but building operations, agricultural activity and, to a lesser extent, domestic and road traffic sources are likely to continue to give rise to high local levels in Greater Manchester in the future.

Isolated measurements of other pollutants apart from smoke and sulphur dioxide have been made in Greater Manchester, including analyses of chrysotile asbestos, chlorine, ethylene and zinc. Measurements of chrysotile asbestos in Rochdale CB (5) using an X-ray diffraction technique revealed that concentrations were below 0.1 $\mu g/m^3$ in the air around a large asbestos factory.[60] Further analyses using electron microscopy[61] revealed that concentrations in the air around the factory, in the centre of Rochdale and on the moors above the town were all in the range $0.1–1.0$ ng/m^3. The difference between the readings at these three locations and those taken at the M5/M6 interchange in Birmingham and at other locations were not significant. It is clear, however, that neither the factory nor motor vehicles are giving rise to chrysotile asbestos concentrations which could constitute a hazard. The industrial Threshold Limit Value is 0.1 mg/m^3, between 5 and 6 orders of magnitude greater than the recorded concentrations.

Zinc analyses similar to those for lead in air showed that Manchester CB (3) had a much lower average annual concentration (0.3 $\mu g/m^3$) than the country as a whole (0.9 $\mu g/m^3$).[56] Similar analyses for copper were inconclusive because the concentrations found were too low to be significant. Certain measurements relating to local sites have also been made. For example, the concentrations of chlorine compounds in the atmosphere in the vicinity of a refuse incinerator burning plastics is being monitored by one local authority.[53] The readings obtained, together with those from a survey of ethylene concentrations in the air around a large industrial site in a local authority in the south west of the sub-region, cannot be taken to be representative of Greater Manchester as a whole.

Measurements of radioactivity in Greater Manchester mainly reflect background radiation and fallout and, apart from a few monitoring points around specific sources, relate to contamination of foodstuffs and tapwater.[62, 63] There have been no measurements of pesticides in the atmosphere of the conurbation but sufficient evidence exists to regard neither pesticides nor radiation, at current levels, as significant environmental pollutants.

Smoke and sulphur dioxide
As in other parts of the country, the data on smoke and sulphur dioxide concentrations in Greater Manchester are far better than those on other pollutants. Daily smoke and sulphur dioxide concentrations have in fact been measured at more than 100 stations in Greater Manchester during the last decade. The sites at which readings were taken were first identified[64] and the peak daily, monthly, summer, winter and yearly mean values were then abstracted from annual statistics.[65] A set of tables, listing readings for about 90 stations for each year, was thus constructed.

A method for comparing average (6 monthly or annual) concentrations[41] was adopted which enabled trends in smoke and sulphur dioxide to be calculated for the conurbation as a whole. Figure 13 shows that average daily winter smoke concentrations have decreased by a factor greater than two within a decade, from well over 300 to around 150 μg/m^3. Summer smoke concentrations have also halved, but these are of much lower magnitude. The annual mean concentrations have accordingly fallen by about 50% over a 10 year period.

A large reduction in winter sulphur dioxide concentrations has also occurred (values having almost halved within a decade). However the fall in summer concentrations has been smaller and the reduction in annual mean values has therefore been about 40% (Figure 14). Annual urban mean concentrations for the UK, the North West region and Salford CB (6) are also shown, the trend being clearly downwards in all cases, with a tendency to approach a similar level. The sulphur dioxide values for Salford, while falling rapidly, illustrate that considerable variations from mean concentrations may occur within the conurbation. The trends in average sulphur dioxide (and other sulphurous gas) levels

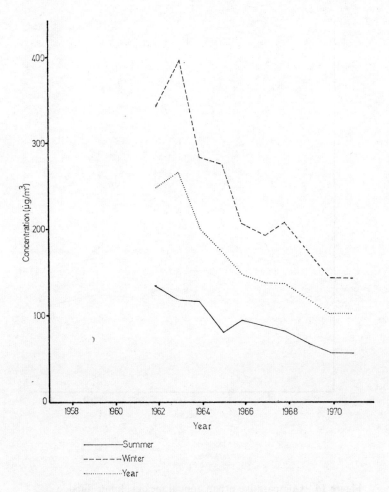

Figure 13 Greater Manchester mean smoke concentrations,
1961–71

obtained by lead dioxide candle measurements closely mirror those
revealed by daily readings.

Although the number of sampling points was too small to construct
accurate contours, it was possible to gather a reasonable impression of
the variation in average concentrations within Greater Manchester for
different years and parts of years for smoke and sulphur dioxide. Figure

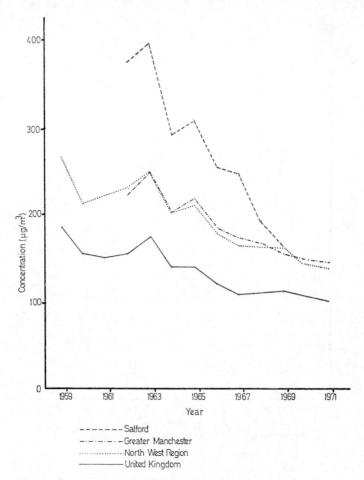

Figure 14   Comparative urban annual mean sulphur dioxide
concentrations, 1958–71

15 shows the average sulphur dioxide situation during the winter of
1963–4, the broad smoke distribution pattern being very similar. How
far the pattern of high central area and low peripheral concentrations
reflects real differences in sulphur dioxide levels between areas cannot be
conclusively established since the absence of readings in a particular
locality does not necessarily mean that pollution concentrations are low.
For example, no readings are available for Wigan CB (8) during this

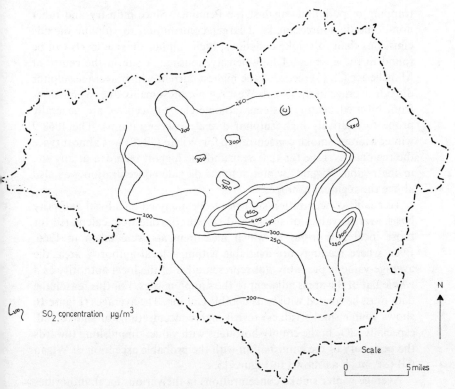

Figure 15 Greater Manchester mean sulphur dioxide concentration contours, winter 1963/4

period but it is likely that concentrations were high. The general pattern is, however, believed to be reasonably correct.

A detailed study of the smoke and sulphur dioxide position in the North West region containing a section on the Greater Manchester area, in which the results at individual stations in 1968/9 and 1969/70 are analysed, has been published.[66] Concentrations of smoke were generally higher north of a line running just south of Eccles MB (12) and Stalybridge MB (22) than those in the area to the south of this line. The same was also true for sulphur dioxide but the distinction was less marked. The main reasons for these differences are probably higher-density housing in the north than in the south, transport of pollutants from the southern and central areas by prevailing winds and trapping of pollutants against the Pennines. Since industry and other non-domestic sources make a larger contribution to sulphur dioxide emissions than to smoke emissions, high sulphur dioxide levels can be found in the absence of high-density housing. A site in the centre of Manchester CB (3) recorded the highest current winter average sulphur dioxide average in the North West region, presumably due to emissions from oil-fired heating systems (commercial city centres are generally prone to relatively high sulphur dioxide concentrations). The 1968/9 winter average smoke concentration for Wigan CB (8) was almost twice the regional average for that year and the highest recorded at any site in the region. Wigan's winter sulphur dioxide concentration was also above the regional average.[66]

To enable concentration statistics to be analysed on a local authority basis, average values of smoke and sulphur dioxide were calculated for those local authorities in which measurements were taken in 1966. Even where readings are available within a local authority area, the average value is probably not representative of the local authority as a whole but of the areas adjacent to the sampling sites. For this reason the data must be treated with considerable caution. The averages (Figure 16 shows winter smoke values) reveal high concentrations of smoke and, especially, SO_2 in the county boroughs with values diminishing towards the periphery of the conurbation with the probable exception of Wigan CB (8), much as shown in Figure 15.

Average winter smoke concentrations in the various local authorities were closely correlated with population density (see Appendix) but the relationship between sulphur dioxide concentrations and population density was less significant ($\alpha = 0.05$). The inverse relationships between both smoke and sulphur dioxide concentrations and car ownership were highly significant, the correlation being even closer when the logarithms of the smoke and sulphur dioxide concentrations were used ($\alpha = 0.0005$). As would be expected, similar relationships between pollutant concentrations and socio-economic grouping index prevailed, the correlation again being better when logarithms of the concentrations were taken. Smoke and sulphur dioxide concentrations were correlated with both total employment and manufacturing employment per acre, the relationships being closest in the case of sulphur dioxide. There was, however, no significant linear correlation between pollutant concentrations and percentage of the area smoke controlled, although this parameter explained some of the variance in several multiple regression equations (see

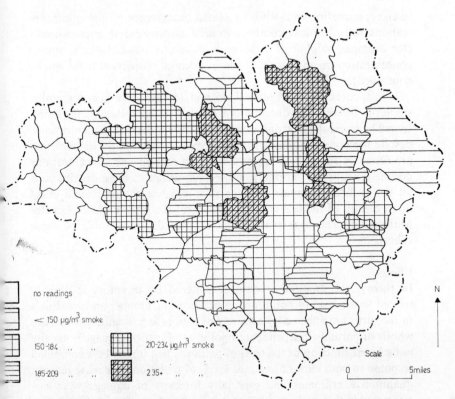

no readings

< 150 μg/m³ smoke

150-184　,,　　,,

185-209　,,　　,,

210-234 μg/m³ smoke

235+　,,　　,,

N

Scale

0　　　　　5miles

Figure 16　Local authority mean smoke concentrations, winter
1965/6

Appendix). Thus, the more densely populated and highly industrialised
areas exhibited the higher smoke and sulphur dioxide concentrations in
1966. These areas tend to be those with the lowest car ownership rates
and the highest socio-economic grouping indices, and the conclusion
may be drawn that the less privileged was the population of a local
authority in 1966, the higher was the air pollution to which it was subject.

On the basis of past trends and known smoke control programmes,[36]
concentrations of smoke and sulphur dioxide should be considerably
lower in 1981 than those which prevail at present. With smoke concentrations expected to fall most rapidly, it appears reasonable to suggest
that daily sulphur dioxide concentrations may average less than
100 μg/m³ and smoke concentrations less than 60 μg/m³ over the year

in the conurbation as a whole. Isolated occurrences of higher concentrations will obviously continue to arise under adverse circumstances (for example, sulphur dioxide levels in certain office districts, smoke concentrations in any residual older residential property still not smoke controlled).

It is apparent from Figures 9, 15 and 16 that there is considerable similarity between the distributions of road traffic pollutants (as represented by traffic density) and smoke and sulphur dioxide concentrations, despite the opposing trends in their levels. In all cases the higher levels are found in the central parts of the conurbation and concentrations decline towards the periphery. As a consequence of these distributions all the pollutants appear to have their greatest environmental effect upon certain of the less affluent sections of the population of Greater Manchester. The next part of the chapter discusses some of these effects.

Effects

In theory, the amount of damage suffered by receptors is directly related to the level of pollution. In practice, the number and condition of receptors are affected by a variety of factors (e.g. weather) which are wholly or partially independent of pollution. Further, damage is usually not a linear function of the level of pollution and it may be a combined response to both current and past levels of pollution. For these reasons quantitative estimates and especially forecasts of damage were not attempted in this study and this section is mainly confined to qualitative evaluations of the effects of smoke and sulphur dioxide (the only pollutants of which reasonably complete measurements on a time series basis have been made) on weather, human health, plants and other receptors.

Weather

The effects of air pollution on climate are mostly attributable to particulate matter. Particulate pollutants suspended in the atmosphere reduce visibility[67] and scatter sunlight, thus diminishing the amount of solar energy reaching the earth's surface.[68] Measurements of both visibility, light intensity and sunshine would therefore be expected to show some relationship with smoke concentrations. As mentioned in Chapter 2, the Weather Centre and the Airport are the main stations recording visibility and sunshine characteristics in Greater Manchester and it was possible to estimate the smoke and sulphur dioxide concentrations at these locations.[69]

Striking improvements in visibility at both meteorological stations are

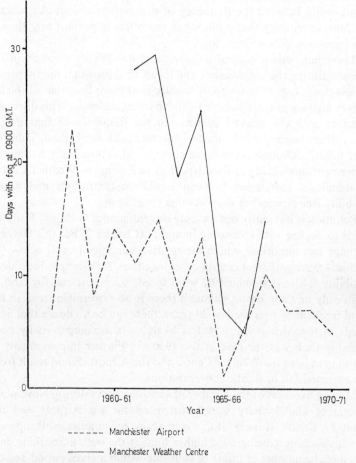

Figure 17 Number of days with fog (visibility < 1000 m) during November–January at Manchester Airport and Weather Centre, 1957–70

plotted in Figure 17. Smoke control programmes have considerably reduced smoke concentrations in the centre of Manchester CB (3) and appear to be partially responsible for the visibility improvements at the Weather Centre, particularly in the case of the less dense fogs. The frequency of fogs (visibility less than 1000 m) during November–January, the winter and the whole year were closely correlated with smoke concentrations (see Appendix). On the other hand, there was no relationship between the frequency of denser fogs and smoke concentrations, confirming that pollution is much less important here than in the formation of less dense fogs.[70]

There has been a general improvement in visibility throughout the country during the last decade[71] and it can be shown that the frequency of less dense fogs at the Airport has declined more than that of thicker fogs (which are not attributable to high particulate levels). This disparity, together with the marked decrease in the frequency of fogs during November–January when smoke concentrations are highest, indicates that falling pollution levels have contributed substantially to the improvement in visibility at the Airport as well as at the Weather Centre. A significant correlation between smoke concentrations and winter visibility (see Appendix) supports this conclusion.

Pollution is obviously not the only determinant of visibility. Visibility tends to decline with increasing humidity (Chapter 2) but this factor is perhaps less important where the relative humidity is well below the national average than at certain other locations, for example Teesside.[72] Visibility is also determined by wind speed, since mist and fog tend to form only on calm days. Although there is no discernible trend in the wind frequencies over the last 20 years, there can be no doubt that light winds at the Airport are now less likely to be accompanied by poor visibility than was the case in the 1950's.[73] Further improvements in visibility at both the Weather Centre and the Airport should result from the expected fall in smoke concentrations.

Moving averages of the number of sunshine hours during November, December and January were constructed for the Airport and the Weather Centre (Figure 18), which show an unmistakable upward trend, values now being 50% higher than at the outset. Sunshine data measure the number of hours of sunshine within a given period and do not indicate the relative strength of the sun's rays. They have nevertheless been found to depend upon smoke pollution concentrations. For example, the increase in the number of hours of sunshine during the months November–January between 1949 and 1970 in Central Manchester is correlated with decreasing smoke concentrations (see Appendix). The increase in sunshine in Bolton CB (1) referred to in Chapter

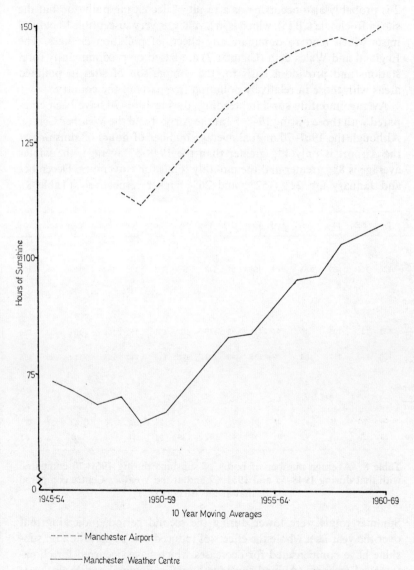

Figure 18 Number of hours of sunshine during November–January at Manchester Airport and Weather Centre, 1945–70

2 is probably also occurring as a result of decreasing pollution but the site in Rochdale CB (5), which is in a valley, is very susceptible to natural mists which tend to dominate any effects of pollution changes. The England and Wales data (Chapter 2) are based on predominantly rural stations and provide a basis for the comparison of sites in polluted areas with those in relatively pollution free parts of the country.

Average monthly sunshine readings during 1961–70 have been compared with those during 1948–57 at the Airport and the Weather Centre. Although the 1961–70 annual average number of hours of sunshine at the Airport is only 1% greater than the 1948–57 average, the winter average is 8% greater and the monthly totals for November, December and January are 22%, 52% and 26% higher respectively (Table 8).

	Jan.	Feb.	Mar.	Apr.	May	June	July	Aug.	Sept.	Oct.	Nov.	Dec.	Year	Sum.	Win.	N - I
Airport																
1961-70 / 1948-57	126	111	89	85	89	108	91	113	104	102	122	152	101	98	108	132
Weather Centre																
1961-70 / 1948-57	152	128	105	98	94	111	93	117	107	121	150	168	109	103	126	156
1961-70 / 1931-57	160	145	117	103	99	115	98	103	105	133	140	188	112	105	136	158
Weather Centre / Airport																
1948-57	60	68	75	81	86	91	91	89	86	79	62	58	82	87	70	60
1961-70	73	79	88	92	91	93	92	92	89	93	76	64	89	92	82	71

Table 8 Average number of hours of sunshine during 1961–70 compared with that during 1948–57 and 1931–67 and at the Weather Centre compared with that at the Airport (%)

Summer totals were lower during the second period, indicating that over the year as a whole the effects of reduced smoke pollution on sunshine have compensated for decreases which have occurred for climatological reasons. (Annual sunshine hours in England and Wales were in fact 5% less during the second period than the first.) The Weather Centre received 9% more sunshine during the year as a whole in the second period and the November, December and January average monthly figures were 50%, 68% and 52% higher respectively. The increased number of hours of sunshine is even more marked if 1961–70 is compared with 1931–57 (Table 8).

Air pollution is only one of many factors affecting the number of hours of sunshine recorded (for example, cloud cover is obviously also important). In addition, long sunny periods often occur paradoxically when temperatures are low, when atmospheric conditions are stable and when light winds prevail, precisely the conditions under which high pollution levels arise,[74] as in 1958, 1961, 1962 and 1964 in Greater Manchester. Nevertheless, the relationship between falling smoke concentrations and rising incidence of sunshine in the conurbation is undeniable. There appears to be no reason why the number of hours of sunshine at the Weather Centre should not be very similar to those at the Airport in the future, given the expected further fall in smoke concentrations.

Human health

Winter smoke and sulphur dioxide concentrations of 250 μg/m³ and 500 μg/m³ respectively have been suggested as thresholds for the exacerbation of chronic bronchitis,[75, 76] a major contributor to morbidity and mortality in the sub-region.[77, 78] Short term exposures to similar or higher concentrations of both pollutants can have an almost immediate, adverse effect upon local mortality rates due mainly to aggravation of bronchitis and emphysema.[79, 80] Within Greater Manchester such a relationship was observed in Manchester CB (3) and Salford CB (6) but great improvements in mortality have occurred in the last ten years.[80] High concentrations (e.g. greater than 300 μg/m³ smoke) are occasionally exceeded in the central and other densely populated local authorities and although these levels used to prevail for considerable periods they now rarely occur for more than a single day at a time. The declining effect of episodic high pollution is confirmed by the fact that average winter concentrations of smoke and sulphur dioxide are now more closely related to mortality than are peak daily concentrations.

A number of studies[81, 82] have shown that human mortality is associated with many non-pollution variables (for example, population density, socio-economic status and income) as well as with pollution. A series of simple regression analyses (see Appendix) was conducted to establish the relationship between current (1969/70) smoke and sulphur dioxide concentrations and other variables with present (1970) mortality rates in Greater Manchester. Mortality amongst males (CMR) and amongst both sexes (AMR) due to bronchitis and emphysema were most closely associated with air pollution. Smoke and sulphur dioxide concentrations were also related to total mortality (TAM) due to all causes. Deaths from bronchitis and emphysema (CMR), lung cancer, hypertensive diseases and ischaemic and other heart diseases correlated with sulphur dioxide concentrations in decreasing order of significance, the associations with prostatic cancer and stomach cancer not being significant. Smoke levels were slightly less closely related to deaths from these diseases than was sulphur dioxide, only the correlation with deaths from bronchitis and emphysema (CMR) being significant.

Current mortality is influenced by exposures to past as well as present pollution concentrations. Thus mortality in 1970 was more closely associated with sulphur dioxide and, especially, smoke concentrations in 1963/4 than with those in 1969/70. In fact, the correlation between total mortality in 1970 and average winter pollution levels declined progressively from 1960 to 1970 (Figure 19). However, of the individual causes of death, only bronchitis and emphysema clearly followed this pattern confirming that deaths from other diseases are strongly influenced by other factors (e.g. lung cancer and smoking[81, 82]) that may themselves be associated with pollution. In general, the relationships between mortality and population density, socio-economic grouping index and car ownership were as strong as those with pollution concentrations.

It has been tentatively estimated that 15–20% of the morbidity and mortality due to bronchitis in the UK is caused by exposure to air pollution over a considerable number of years.[83] Given the above average incidences of this disease and above average levels of pollution in the North West, a realistic proportion for Greater Manchester might be $20 \pm 5\%$, equivalent to perhaps 400–650 deaths per annum.

The relationships between current mortality levels in individual authorities and smoke and sulphur dioxide concentrations in various years, socio-economic status of population and its density were also analysed by multiple regression techniques (see Appendix). Problems were, however, encountered because certain of the explanatory variables were correlated with each other as well as with mortality. The most important explanatory variables were socio-economic grouping index followed by population density and smoke and sulphur dioxide pollution levels. In fact, pollution levels and population density were not always significant but historic (1963/4) concentrations, especially of smoke, seemed more closely related to current mortality than were current concentrations.

Smoke and sulphur dioxide concentrations should become less significant in determining morbidity and mortality rates as they decrease.[81, 84] The same may not be true of the effects of vehicle emissions [1]

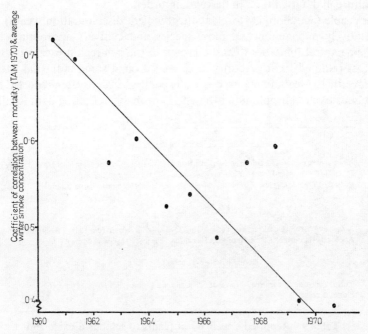

Figure 19 Relationship between Greater Manchester mortality, 1970, and mean winter smoke concentrations 1969/70 and preceding years

and in particular of lead. The relationship between the relatively high concentrations of this metal recorded in parts of the Greater Manchester and current body burdens is unknown. It is apparent, however, that increases in the levels of lead in blood are undesirable (especially in children[85]) and that such increases may be anticipated in the most polluted areas unless future emissions from motor vehicles and other sources are controlled.

Plants

Sulphur dioxide and smoke, together with sulphur acid aerosols, are probably the main pollutants causing plant damage in Greater Manchester although some local effects are attributed to other forms of pollution (e.g. ethylene, road salt sprays, iron oxide, cement dust). The major types of receptors were identified by Parks and Cemetery Superintendents[86] as ornamental plants and tree plantations, horticulture and agriculture, in descending order.

Visible (acute) injury to plants (e.g. violent discolouration, death) is relatively uncommon and most species and cultivars appropriate to their natural limitations can be grown in the sub-region except in the most polluted local authority areas and around some industrial sites. Nevertheless, certain plants, especially conifers,[88] were often reported to be sensitive to air pollution (Table 9),[86] probably reflecting both locally

---

Sensitive Species and Cultivars

Most evergreens and conifers (especially Larix), Fagus, Aesculus, Catalpa, Prunus (especially Plum), Viburnum, Liriodendron, Magnolia, Bush fruits (e.g. gooseberry), Lucerne, Aubretia, Myosotis, Grasses (some), Rosa (some).

Less Sensitive

A few evergreens and conifers (including Cupressus), Acer (excluding Sycamore), Apple, Silver Birch, Rosa (some), Veronica (some), Grasses (some).

Insensitive or Tolerant

Tulip, Rowan, Sycamore, Blackberry, Grasses (some), Clovers (some), Plane, Privet.

Table 9   Reported sensitivity of plants to sulphur dioxide and smoke pollution in Greater Manchester

acute and more widespread forms of cryptic injury (e.g. reduced growth, early senescence, establishment failure, etc.) due to exposure to sublethal concentrations of sulphur dioxide and perhaps to other pollutants. [87]

Damage was reported mostly in local authorities where average sulphur dioxide concentrations exceeded 95, 130 and 300 $\mu g/m^3$ in summer, during the year and in winter respectively.[86] Peak concentrations exceeding 400 $\mu g/m^3$ for periods of one day or less can be expected in many such areas with the possibility of some associated visible injury to very sensitive plants.[89] However, most damage to plants in the Greater Manchester sub-region is probably the result of cryptic injuries following prolonged exposures to much lower concentrations (50–300 μg/m³) of sulphur dioxide.[90]

In order to make crude estimates of some agricultural and other plant losses due to air pollution in Greater Manchester, it was assumed that visible injury due to peak daily concentrations of 200–400 and more than 400 μg/m³ of sulphur dioxide resulted in yield losses of 1% and 5% respectively. Cryptic injury was assumed to result in losses of 10% and 25% at average summer concentrations of sulphur dioxide of 75–124 and 125–175 μg/m³ respectively. No allowances were made for winter exposures, for sulphur deficiencies,[91] for compensatory growth by less sensitive plants or for differences in management regimes. Table 10

Receptors	% Yield Loss/annum	Acreage Equivalent	Yield Equivalent (tons/annum)	Crude Estimated Losses £000's
All grasslands (all sensitive)	8.6	8100	12,500	450-500
All grasslands (30% sensitive)	2.6	2480	3,730	170
All agricultural pastures (30% sensitive)	2.3	1920	3,180	130
Agricultural seeded pastures (30% sensitive)	2.2	1870	3,070	115
Cereals (all sensitive)	4.6	940	1,360	35
Cereals (30% sensitive)	1.4	295	430	10
Potatoes (50% sensitive)	2.7	67	635	10

Table 10 Estimated losses of plant productivity due to sulphur dioxide pollution in Greater Manchester, 1970

contains rough estimates of replacement and yield[92] losses for cereals and for grasslands (pastures,[31] rough grazing,[31] parks, golfcourses,[32,33] etc. but excluding private lawns and verges) assuming (a) that all plants are sensitive and (b) that only 30% of plants are sensitive. Additional estimates of losses are provided for all agricultural grasslands, seed pastures and potatoes assuming partial sensitivity to sulphur dioxide. All other crops are excluded because they constitute only 3% of the total cultivated acreage in the sub-region,[31] although their market value is considerable. However, yield losses to all forms of agricultural, horti-cultural and ornamental plants in Greater Manchester at 1970 product sale prices may well exceed £1m (including replacement costs, etc.) of which about half probably arises from damage to grasslands. However, further research is needed to obtain a more precise estimate.

The reductions in smoke and especially sulphur dioxide levels during the last decade have led to improvements in the growth of conifers close to the sub-region and in general to decreasing plant damage over the last 5 years.[86] It is also possible that falling smoke pollution has con-tributed to these improvements indirectly by increasing the number of hours of sunshine and light intensity, thus promoting better growth. Provided that concentrations of photo-oxidant pollutants, which are known to damage plants,[89] do not increase significantly the effects of air pollution on plants are expected to continue to diminish.

Other effects
There is little detailed information about damage to materials in Greater Manchester although 86% of local authority Parks and Cemetery Superintendents replying to questionnaires[86] reported corrosion and soiling of the structures within their jurisdiction by air pollution (80% of those authorities reporting damage had peak current daily concen-trations of sulphur dioxide and smoke of at least 750 and 500 $\mu g/m^3$ respectively). It is known that zinc corrodes about 60% faster in the industrial parts of the conurbation than on its Cheshire perimeter.[93] On the basis of other corrosion studies,[94] it can be estimated that current levels of sulphur dioxide may increase the corrosion of metals (e.g. mild steel) and stonework (especially limestone) by 50–70% in many central, northern and eastern local authorities compared with cleaner, rural areas. Soiling by particulates is probably less, adding perhaps 10–25% to maintenance costs (e.g. cleansing of buildings, fabrics, etc.) in certain authorities. The reduction in smoke pollution has influenced the cleaning of many buildings in Greater Manchester in recent years, much of the cost involved in cleansing being attributable to restoring materials either damaged directly by pollution or by removing the accumulated effects of air pollution in previous years. In general, effects on materials may be expected to decline with decreasing smoke and sulphur dioxide pollution although local problems, mainly due to industrial emissions and motor vehicles, may remain.

Evidence of air pollution effects on stock, domestic and wild animals in Greater Manchester is lacking with the exception of very localised incidents involving damage to cattle by industrial pollutants and some studies of melanism in moths. In the latter case there has been an apparent decline in populations of melanic forms of certain species concomitant with decreases in atmospheric smoke concentrations.[95] As in Greater London, some species of raptorial birds (e.g. kestrels) are returning to the central part of the conurbation, with the improvement in the atmospheric and other environmental conditions. A likely effect of further falls in smoke and sulphur dioxide concentrations is that a greater diversity of bird species may be found in the sub-region in the future.[96]

An assessment of the severity of air pollution and its effects in the various local authorities was obtained from questionnaires completed by Chief Public Health Inspectors.[53] In the Inspectors' opinions domestic fires, followed by industry, were the most important sources of air pollution, probably reflecting in part their statutory responsibilities for these emissions. The most frequent causes for complaint about air pollution to Public Health Inspectors in the sub-region were industry and domestic sources, in that order. There were also a few complaints about road traffic pollutants. The trend in complaints about air pollution was generally downwards (in contrast to complaints about noise —Chapter 6). Numbers of complaints per thousand population about industrial and domestic sources of air pollution reflected differences in manufacturing industrial activity and residential density respectively in the local authorities concerned. There were, however, no generally significant correlations between numbers of complaints per thousand population about road traffic pollution and vehicle densities, between complaints about all types of air pollution and smoke or sulphur dioxide concentrations, or between complaints about all types of air pollution and the affluence of the local authorities concerned.

The Inspectors felt on balance that industry, agriculture and sewage works were equally important as odour sources within Greater Manchester. On the other hand, complaints from the public about odours from domestic premises were most frequent followed by those about industry—the numbers of both probably increasing over the conurbation as a whole. There appeared to be little relationship between the numbers of complaints about odours from industrial, domestic and agricultural sources and the level of these activities in particular local authorities and there was no indication that a particular income group was registering more complaints than the others.[53]

It seems that complaints to Public Health Inspectors only partially reflect the known repercussions of the air pollution process in Greater Manchester. Thus, numbers of complaints from the public do not appear to give a reliable indication of either the pollution resulting from the emissions of waste within the sub-region described in this chapter, or of its effects.

4 Land pollution

Land pollution is perhaps normally thought to be synonymous with soil pollution caused by the permeation of heavy metal, pesticide, fertiliser and other wastes into the soil. However, solid or semi-solid wastes deposited on land to form heaps or tips which damage plants, health, amenity etc. also give rise to land pollution. It is with the latter type of pollution—land pollution from solid wastes—that this chapter is concerned.

The chapter considers these various types of waste and the pollution and damage to which their disposal gives rise. In general, however, considerably more information is available about the wastes than about the resultant pollution. As in the case of air-borne wastes, it is convenient to classify solid wastes by source (i.e. refuse, industrial wastes, sewage sludge, agricultural wastes and mineral working wastes) rather than by their precise constituents, which are frequently common to more than one source. The wastes which comprise derelict spoil heaps and tips and litter of themselves constitute pollution and are therefore dealt with separately.

Refuse

Refuse consists mainly of cinder, dust, vegetable and putrescible matter, paper, metal, rag, glassware and plastics collected by local authorities from domestic and 'trade' (i.e. small commercial businesses, shops or restaurants) premises. Over the country as a whole, amounts of cinder and dust in refuse are falling rapidly, but the proportions of all the other constituents are increasing.[97] A number of studies of refuse disposal within groups of local authorities in Greater Manchester have been made.[98–101] Using these studies together with official statistics[102] and questionnaire returns[103] the daily amount of refuse collected from domestic and trade premises in nearly every local authority area was determined. Unfortunately, there was often considerable disagreement between the figures derived from two or more sources, a reflection of the general dearth of accurate refuse disposal statistics.[97] In Greater Manchester as a whole about one million tons of refuse were probably collected during 1970. In addition, at least 2500 abandoned vehicles were either removed from the streets or received by local authorities.

The quantity of refuse collected in a particular local authority was closely related to its population, although the tonnage collected per thousand population varied from about 0·6 to 4·6 tons per year. The actual amount would be expected to depend upon the socio-economic characteristics of a local authority and upon the types of dwellings and heating methods, and the degree of smoke control prevailing there.[104] However, because of the unreliable nature of the statistics (due partly to local variations in collection practices and partly to the absence of weighing facilities) no significant relationship could be established between the quantity of refuse and these explanatory variables. An additional factor in refuse generation is the employment pattern in the area, since the working population of any local authority will generate a considerable quantity of refuse but neither could a relationship be established with this explanatory variable, probably for the same reasons.

The method of disposal of refuse within Greater Manchester varies from one authority to another. Of the 53 local authorities disposing of refuse in Greater Manchester for which 1970 information was available,[98-101, 103] 46 tipped the waste directly on to land. Of the remainder, four tipped some refuse but incinerated the majority, one tipped part of the refuse and pulverised the remainder, one incinerated all refuse and one pulverised all refuse. The residues from incineration and pulverisation were also tipped.

The number and acreages of active refuse tips were obtained for the local authorities within Greater Manchester.[53, 103, 105-107] The sizes of the 60–70 active tips varied from 0·5–35 acres and on average made up 0·25% of the areas of local authorities (Table 11[107]). The Department of the Environment recommendations for the control of refuse tipping[108] are followed to a varying extent at these tips. It appears that about 5% of the local authorities tipping refuse follow the recommendations faithfully, 40% very closely, 50% quite closely and 5% not at all.[103] Three hundred of the total of about 900 acres of tips in Greater Manchester are covered by planning conditions considered likely to ensure satisfactory after-treatment once tipping has ceased.

The pollution and consequent damage from the disposal of refuse depends upon the manner and site of disposal and upon the use of surrounding land.[109] Although incineration converts solid wastes into gaseous and particulate air-borne wastes, the pollution resulting from normal operation is not usually significant. On the other hand, the pollution arising from tipping untreated refuse, and possibly from tipping pulverised wastes, depends upon the way the operation is conducted. Some nuisance from tipping operations is unavoidable but, in principle, a well-controlled tip should not give rise to air, water or severe land pollution.[97] Once operations have ceased, it is quite possible to reclaim tipping land for other uses satisfactorily.

It is therefore difficult to identify the distinction between waste, pollution and damage in the case of refuse tips. The waste, refuse, is deposited upon land and, provided that it is treated properly,[108] there should be no damage and hence no pollution. If, on the other hand, the waste is not properly controlled, the tip may itself constitute land pollution since it damages the amenity of the surrounding area.

A poorly controlled tip can give rise to such air pollution problems as odours, wind-blown material or particulate matter. (Noise from vehicles and mechanical operations may also arise.) Rain water percolating through tips can cause river pollution and there may possibly be some hazard to public health.[110] Tipping sites also obliterate wildlife habitats and may cause other damage to animals. However, no quantitative data relating to these effects are available.

An analysis of complaints about odours, dust and wind-blown material from tips in local authorities in Greater Manchester[53, 103] showed clearly that numbers of complaints were related to the degree of control exercised. Poor tip location is responsible for a number of continuous polluting discharges to water courses in the conurbation,[111] but occasional water pollution incidents appear to be related to the degree of tip control in force.[103] Damage to visual amenity appears to depend mainly on the degree of control but it was not possible to estimate this effect either from a knowledge of the level of control or from the size of the tip. A few animals have been killed in Greater Manchester by suffocation or ingestion of plastics, toxic materials, etc.,[86] but the number of deaths could not be related to the quantities of refuse tipped or to the manner of site operation.

Forecasts of quantities of refuse depend upon a large number of factors, including future population, affluence, packaging and heating patterns.[97, 112] Questionnaires returned by 28 local authorities indicated that little change in the quantity of refuse was expected by 1981, although its volume was expected to increase considerably.[103] On a

Local Authority Number	Derelict Spoil Heaps & Tips	Active Mineral Spoil Heaps	Active Tips			TOTAL Spoil Heaps & Tips	% Area Occupied
			Local Authority	Industrial	Local Authority & Industrial		
1	31.8	-	23.7	-	-	55.5	0.9
2	12.0	-	-	-	-	12.0	0.4
3	27.9	15.5	108.8	6.0	-	158.2	1.4
4	21.2	-	3.0	0.3	-	24.5	1.0
5	1.6	-	8.9	11.5	-	22.0	0.6
6	-	-	-	0.4	-	0.4	0
7	5.5	-	11.3	35.0	0.6	52.4	1.5
8	50.1	-	-	-	-	50.1	2.4
9							
10	26.2	-	1.1	-	-	27.3	1.6
11	4.8	-	-	-	-	4.8	0.7
12	18.9	-	0.2	3.8	-	22.9	1.7
13	5.2	0.5	5.6	-	-	11.3	1.9
14	18.0	1.8	3.4	11.6	0.4	35.2	1.0
15	-	-	-	-	-	0	0
16	146.4	-	19.9	68.7	-	235.0	9.1
17	6.4	-	-	. -	4.0	10.4	0.5
18	14.9	0.8	4.7	-	-	20.4	1.4
19	1.9	-	3.9	0.6	-	6.4	0.7
20	49.6	-	-	43.8	-	93.4	4.7
21							
22	-	-	-	-	-	0	0
23	25.9	-	8.5	5.6	-	40.0	2.8
24	65.5	-	14.7	65.2	-	145.4	10.7
25	35.8	21.0	1.4	-	-	58.2	7.3
26	1.2	-	-	-	-	1.2	0.2
27	68.6	-	3.4	-	-	72.0	7.9
28	7.1	-	5.3	-	-	12.4	2.5
29	4.9	-	7.3	1.3	-	13.5	1.4
30							
31	8.9	-	-	-	-	8.9	0.5
32	6.8	-	7.3	0.9	-	15.0	1.2
33	-	-	-	-			
34	21.0	-	3.3	1.2	-	25.5	2.2
35	16.7	-	8.2	0.2	-	25.1	2.4
36	26.9	-	6.4	-	-	33.3	6.6

Table 11 Areas of active refuse, industrial and mineral spoil tips and derelict spoil heaps and tips (hectares) and proportion of land occupied by local authority, 1972

national scale the weight of refuse per household is likely to increase by about 10% by 1980, whereas the volume will probably grow much more rapidly as the proportion of paper and plastic becomes larger.[97] Detailed investigations of future refuse quantities in two groups of local authori-

Local Authority Number	Derelict Spoil Heaps & Tips	Active Mineral Spoil Heaps	Active Tips Local Authority	Industrial	Local Authority & Industrial	TOTAL Spoil Heaps & Tips	% Area Occupied
37	13.4	-	4.8	1.2	-	19.4	-
38							
39	-	-	-	-	-	0	0
40	24.9	-	6.5	-	-	31.4	3.0
41	33.2	-	-	0.9	-	34.1	2.6
42	93.0	-	6.7	8.9	-	108.6	11.6
43	20.7	-	-	-	-	20.7	1.1
44	2.4	-	-	1.7	-	4.1	0.6
45	18.1	-	2.4	0.6	-	.21.1	18.2
46	6.2	-	2.7	0.2	-	9.1	0.3
47	8.2	-	1.4	2.0	-	11.6	3.6
48	-	-	-	-	-	0	0
49	-	-	-	-	-		
50	11.6	-	-	-	-	11.6	0.6
51							
52	24.2	-	0.2	0.4	1.6	26.4	3.0
53	16.6	-	-	-	-	16.6	0.2
54	40.5	-	5.2	-	-	45.7	3.5
55	2.8	-	-	-	-	2.8	0.3
56	186.9	-	-	1.2	-	188.1	9.0
57	24.3	-	2.4	4.8	-	31.5	1.6
58	9.0	-	2.6	-	-	11.6	0.9
59	59.9	-	7.4	-	-	67.3	3.0
60	16.4	-	2.2	-	-	18.6	1.4
61							
62							
63	54.3	-	38.6	1.3	-	94.2	3.2
64	30.0	-	-	-	-	30.0	1.2
65	6.9	7.6	-	-	-	14.5	0.5
66	7.2	-	-	0.1	-	7.3	0.4
67	13.7	23.6	5.3	2.2	-	44.8	1.2
68	9.6	3.2	-	0.6	-	13.4	0.3
69	6.1	-	2.2	-	-	8.3	0.1
70	-	-				0	0
71							
TOTAL	1471.8	74.0	350.9	282.2	6.6	2185.5	1.57

Table 11 (cont.)

ties[98, 99, 113] in Greater Manchester forecast weight increases of 17% and 27% between 1969 and 1981. It thus seems unlikely that total quantities collected in the Greater Manchester area as a whole will be less than 1·3 million tons per annum by 1981.

The pollution to which this refuse will give rise depends upon the method of disposal because tipping tends to be much less expensive than

other methods of refuse disposal, and this in turn largely depends on
the amount of land available for tipping within the conurbation.
Greater Manchester can be roughly divided into four geographical
areas with respect to tip life. The western authorities appear to have
enough suitable land likely to be available for refuse tipping for another
20 years and the central, southern and the northern and eastern local
authorities for about 10 years, 5–8 years and 2–3 years respectively.
Many of these authorities will consequently be forced to use alternative
methods of disposal such as incineration or long distance haulage of
refuse[114] by 1981, which will probably give rise to less pollution than
tipping. It is probable that many small tips will be closed by 1981 and
that any new tips will be subject to more rigorous planning control
governing both operation and after-treatment.[108] The total land
pollution resulting from refuse disposal activities thus seems certain to
diminish in the future.

Industrial wastes

Far less information was obtainable about wastes from manufacturing
industry than about refuse. Details of the solid and non-effluent liquid
wastes generated by a limited number of firms in the conurbation were
available,[115] however. These showed that liquid industrial wastes
derived mainly from the chemical industry (petro-chemicals, heavy
organic chemicals, plastics, detergents, etc.). These, together with glue,
paper and textile wastes, appear to make up about 95% of the total
quantity of liquid waste tankered away from industrial premises by
contractors, equivalent to approximately 3% by volume of the trade
effluent treated at sewage works. The wastes are apparently deposited at
certain tips outside Greater Manchester and, to a lesser extent, at sea.
The chemical industry is similarly the main generator of solid wastes[115]
which are mostly tipped at sites both within and outside the conurbation. The considerable quantity of pulverised fuel ash arising within
Greater Manchester is all sold for re-use and does not cause significant
land pollution.[116] Small quantities of radioactive wastes, generated
primarily by industrial, research, educational and medical establish-
ments are occasionally buried in local authority tips within the conurbation.[53] A regular, carefully controlled, collection and disposal
service is operated to remove radioactive wastes from users in Manchester CB (3).

A survey of industrial wastes in the large trading estate in Stretford

MB (23) and Urmston UD (57)[100] revealed that about 760,000 tons of industrial waste were generated in 1969. A few large concerns are responsible for most of the waste, with the chemicals, brick and construction and metals industries (in that order) giving rise to most waste per employee. About 135,000 tons of waste are combustible, and most of the remainder is inert, consisting mainly of slag, excavated material, lime fines, ash, clinker brick and concrete. In addition, approximately 190,000 tons of hazardous waste (mostly liquids) which are toxic or caustic or both are removed by contractors—presumably to be tipped together with most of the other non-combustible waste.[100] The use of manufacturing employment data (Chapter 2) to obtain a comparable figure for the whole of Greater Manchester indicates that roughly 10 million tons of industrial waste are created each year, very much more than the domestic total. Over the country as a whole, it has been estimated that the quantity of industrial waste just exceeds that of refuse,[109] and the concentration of large firms in Trafford Park suggests that the conurbation total is an over-estimate.

It is known that tipping by both producers and contractors, incineration and marine dumping are all employed to deal with Greater Manchester's industrial waste. Unfortunately, information about disposal is limited to the acreages of land used for tipping in various local authorities.[105, 107] The number of tips (about 70) is similar to that of refuse tips but the acreage of land employed is slightly smaller (about 700 acres, or 0·2% of the total conurbation acreage (Table 11[107])). Significantly fewer industrial waste tips are subject to planning conditions than are local authority tips, only about 60 acres being controlled in this way in Greater Manchester. It appears that some of the large tips in the western part of the conurbation may consist of mineral spoil rather than of industrial waste (Table 11). If these are excluded, the total tip acreage falls to about 300, or less than 0·1% of the area of Greater Manchester as a whole.[105, 107] No information about the degree of tip control and hence about pollution (or indeed about pollution from other methods of industrial waste disposal) is available.

The damage caused by industrial waste tips in Greater Manchester is similar to that caused by refuse disposal. Because the proportion of inert materials is smaller, however, the likelihood of water pollution is greater. Significant pollution arises from certain tips[111] and, in addition, a number of polluting incidents occurs each year, many of which are due to inadequate tip supervision.[12] Despite the wind-blown dispersal of, for example, metallic and other tipped dusts, industrial waste tips do not generally appear to be major contributors to atmospheric pollution.

There were far fewer public complaints to local authorities about this type of tip than about refuse tips (probably reflecting the lack of direct authority control), although significant numbers of complaints about wind-blown material, dusts and odours were received.[53, 103] The pre-eminent effect of industrial waste disposal again seems to be loss of amenity, although the possibility of contaminating soils or water is always present.

Forecasting the quantities of industrial waste likely to be produced is obviously difficult, beyond stating that an increase appears likely. However, stricter planning controls over new tips[108] and new legislation (for example, the Deposit of Poisonous Waste Act 1972) would reduce the pollution resulting from the disposal of these wastes in the future, if they are operated effectively and reflected in better site management.

Sewage sludge

Sewage sludge consists of grit, 'primary' sludge deposited in sedimentation tanks and 'secondary' sludge resulting from the biological treatment processes at sewage treatment plants. The thick liquid (although only semi-solid it is normally considered a land pollutant) comprises about $\frac{1}{2}$–1% of the initial volume of sewage.[117]

At most works sludge is treated by air drying on beds or lagooning. About 1·4 million tons of sewage sludge are generated in Greater Manchester each year, the solid content of which varies from about 3 to 75%, but probably averages about 5%.[118] The resulting 70,000 tons dry weight is thus equivalent to about 25 tons per person per year, similar to the national average.[119]

The most frequently used method of sludge disposal in Greater Manchester is spraying or spreading on land, although this method only accounted for 15% of the total weight generated. Several sewage works sold sludge to gardeners and farmers (50% of that spread on land or 7·5% of the total quantity). The disposal of sludge at drying areas within the works perimeter and at tips outside the works are the next most frequently employed methods of disposal (both 11% of the total). Although only utilised by a few works, sea disposal accounted for 60% of the total quantity of sludge or about 40,000 tons dry weight per annum.[118, 120] Two works employed waste disposal contractors to remove sludge and were not aware of its eventual method of disposal.[118]

The urban nature of Greater Manchester and the shortage of tipping space is emphasised by comparison with the country as a whole, where it is estimated that 20% of sludge is dumped at sea, 40% is applied to agricultural land and 40% is disposed of on land in other ways (tipping, lagooning, etc.).[117]

The disposal of sewage sludge on land can be associated with odour and water pollution, but no information about pollution or damage in Greater Manchester could be obtained. The export of sewage sludge to Liverpool Bay has been the subject of an investigation which reported only very limited damage to the environment.[120]

The quantities of sewage sludge generated in Greater Manchester are likely to increase with rising water usage, the utilisation of such domestic appliances as sink disposal units and the tightening of controls on effluents to rivers. Stricter water pollution control is likely both to divert trade effluent to sewage works and to increase the efficiency of treatment, leading to a growth in quantities of sludge remaining. It has been forecast that the annual amount of sewage sludge from Greater Manchester dumped in Liverpool Bay may increase to over 100,000 tons by the mid-1970s but it was thought unlikely that the long term effects of these disposals would be significant,[120] a conclusion which has not been universally accepted.

Agricultural wastes
Agricultural holdings both utilise and generate wastes. About 750 tons of abbatoir wastes, together with large tonnages of fertilisers and pesticides, 3500 dry tons of sewage sludge and 2500 tons of animal slurry are applied to agricultural land in Greater Manchester each year.[86, 118] The quantities of waste generated are much greater, however. Loadings of wastes were calculated for each animal species (cattle, horses, sheep, goats, pigs and poultry) in each local authority[31] using waste coefficients[121] and assumptions about horse and unregistered pig and poultry populations.[92] The total amount of animal waste generated in the conurbation is estimated to be about 280 million gallons of slurry annually (1970–1) containing approximately 5800 tons of nitrogen and 1000 tons of phosphorus. By way of comparison the equivalent human loadings— faeces and detergents—are about 6000 tons of nitrogen and 2400 tons of phosphorus. There are additional unquantified urban run-off, industrial and natural sources of these elements in Greater Manchester.

As would be expected, estimates of the quantities of agricultural waste

per acre in the various local authorities are inversely related to human
population density (see Appendix). There is, however, no clear relationship between waste loadings and the number of persons employed in
agriculture, probably because the different types of agriculture practised
in Greater Manchester (e.g. market gardening, pig rearing) have both

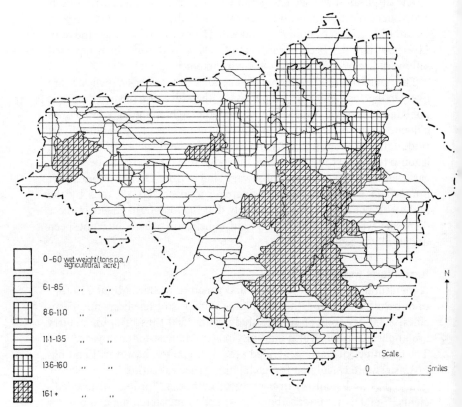

0 -6·0 wet weight (tons p.a. /
           agricultural acre)

6·1-8·5   „   „

8·6-11·0   „   „

11·1-13·5   „   „

13·6-16·0   „   „

16·1 +   „   „

N

Scale

0   5 miles

Figure 20   Local authority animal wastes, 1970/1

different waste characteristics and different labour requirements. Waste
loadings per agricultural acre (Figure 20), on the other hand, are positively correlated with human population density, indicating that
intensive farming (for example, pigs and poultry with resulting
phosphorus-rich wastes) accompanies increasing demand for land in the
more central local authorities (see Appendix). In general, waste loadings

could not be related to the socio-economic characteristics of the Greater Manchester local authorities. In the northern authorities, however, loadings are highest in the lower-income rural areas, whereas loadings rise with income (as measured by socio-economic grouping index) in the southern authorities where suburban residential areas and agriculture appear not to be in conflict with each other.

The main pollution problem associated with agricultural wastes is run-off to rivers. Total quantities of nitrogen and phosphorus draining to rivers from fertilisers, animals and humans may be estimated, using a number of assumptions, to be more than 32,000 tons of nitrate and about 5100 tons of phosphate per annum, of which human wastes contribute the greatest proportion. No run-off total for pesticides could be derived. The relationship between estimated loadings and the re-sulting pollution and damage is obscure, although it is possible that loadings per agricultural acre give an indication of disposal and hence pollution and damage problems. Indeed the relationship between animal nitrogen per agricultural acre and river quality is just significant ($\alpha = 0.05$). Evidence of damage is confined to episodic fish kills, caused by accidental discharges of pesticides and farm effluents.[12] For example, severe organic river pollution due to piggeries has occurred in Droylsden UD (36) and Failsworth UD (37), which both have high waste loadings.

Forecasts of animal wastes depend upon future land use changes in Greater Manchester, the growth of agricultural activity and changes in farming methods and waste disposal techniques. Assuming little change apart from a 7–11% increase in animal wastes due to increased stock rearing over the next decade,[122] the total dry weight of wastes could reach 120–150,000 tons per annum (equivalent to about 1150 tons of phosphorus). Should this be attributable to increased intensification it is probable that waste disposal problems will grow, giving rise to some water pollution and local odour pollution.

Mineral working wastes

Coal spoil is the major type of waste from active mineral workings in Greater Manchester. There are at present four pits operating in the conurbation producing about 1·25 million tons of spoil each year, of which about 0·25 million tons is utilised for construction purposes.[123] Net annual production of this waste from underground mines is thus approximately 1·0 million tons. The spoil is tipped at 6 sites in local authorities to the west of the conurbation, covering about 90 acres in all. Two of the tips are not subject to planning conditions and although the remaining four sites are covered, the local planning authority (Lancashire County Council) considers the conditions inadequate to secure satisfactory reclamation once tipping has ceased.[105]

Sandstone and clay have now overtaken coal as the most important minerals extracted in Greater Manchester in terms of the acreage of active workings.[105, 107] There are about 60 acres of spoil heaps at active sandstone quarries in the Pennine foothills, i.e. in the local authorities to the north and east of the sub-region. The other minerals worked in the conurbation, brick clay and sand, do not always give rise to spoil heaps, but considerable acreages of clay waste heaps occur in Manchester CB (3) and Golborne UD (65) as can be seen from Table 11.[107] Difficulties in calculating precise acreages arise from the use of mineral working sites for domestic and industrial waste tipping, but it appears that there are about 200 acres of active mineral spoil heaps at 11 sites in the conurbation. About 70 acres of this total are subject to planning conditions specifying restoration.[105, 107] It seems likely that the reclamation of at least four of the coal spoil heaps will be accomplished although the standard of the reclaimed land may well be unsatisfactory to the local planning authority.[105, 123] The same is probably true where sandstone and other types of mineral spoil heap are to be reclaimed by the operator.

It is probable that spoil heaps at active workings of themselves constitute pollution since the large quantities of waste involved normally affect visual amenity whether or not after-treatment is intended. Certainly, any tip which is inadequately reclaimed represents a long-term pollution problem. There have been no dangerous tip slips in Greater Manchester[124] apart from occasional lagoon collapses and since none of the active coal tips are burning, air pollution arises only from surface dust. The high acidity[125] and suspended solids content of the run-off from tips together with some discolouration due to iron[111] may cause local pollution of water courses. As in the case of domestic tips, however, damage to amenity is probably the most important effect.

The increasing re-use of colliery spoil and the possible diminution in coal mining activity in the conurbation indicate that future quantities of tipped coal spoil will be smaller than at present. Conversely, the construction industry is expected to require increased quantities of sandstone and other minerals, in addition to mining wastes, and more spoil will probably be generated in supplying this demand. In both cases, new workings are certain to be subject to much more rigorous planning conditions relating to spoil tipping and reclamation than in the past. There is thus likely to be less land pollution and damage from mineral wastes in 1981 than at present, although problems at certain existing workings may grow.

Derelict spoil heaps and tips
Derelict waste heaps and litter can be distinguished from those wastes which may or may not of themselves be polluting. Derelict land is officially described as land so damaged by industrial or other development that it is 'incapable of beneficial use without treatment'.[126] Where dereliction arises from the disposal of solid wastes which cause damage (for example, to amenity) it must, by definition, constitute pollution. This is the case with derelict spoil heaps and tips.

Local authorities return statistics relating to the acreage of spoil heaps and other types of dereliction in their areas to the Department of the Environment annually, and these show an overall increase during the last few years in Greater Manchester (Table 12[127]). However, because

Year	Acreage
1966	2275
1967	2302
1968	2461
1969	2573
1970	2548

Table 12 Area of officially classified derelict spoil heaps in Greater Manchester, 1966–70

of varying interpretations of the definition, these figures are generally regarded as unreliable and thus cannot be used to give an accurate indication of trends. The scope of the derelict land survey is to be widened in 1974, when it will cover additional categories of industrially scarred land (the reclamation of which is not subject to government grants) and 'despoiled' land, i.e. land used for mineral working and waste tipping.[128]

The local planning authorities have surveyed derelict land in their areas in considerable detail.[105-107, 129] From their results it appears that the total acreage of derelict spoil heaps and tips in Greater Manchester in 1970/1 was approximately 3700 acres or 1·0% of the overall area compared with about 0·15% of the area of England.[130] (The total acreage of derelict land—including buildings, excavations, etc.—in the conurbation was about 8100 acres or 2·2% of the total area.)

The total number of derelict spoil heaps and tips in Greater Manchester is about 450, the vast majority of which are small, a few very large sites accounting for a great proportion of the total acreage. Derelict industrial and domestic tips are very widespread and difficult to distinguish from each other. About 25% of the total acreage of derelict spoil heaps and tips falls in this category, the mean size of 150–200 sites being about 6 acres. Colliery spoil comprises about 60% of the total acreage of derelict spoil heaps, the mean size of approximately 200 derelict colliery spoil tips being 11 acres. Sandstone spoil makes up the remaining 15% of the total acreage with a site size of 7·5 acres.

Statistics for the acreage of derelict spoil heaps and tips for each local authority were also obtained from the surveys.[105–107, 129] The results showed a very considerable variation when acreages were calculated as a proportion of the total area of each local authority. Table 11 shows that derelict spoil heaps and tips comprise more than 4% of several authority areas, although only Ince-in-Makerfield UD (42), Lees UD (45) and Tyldesley UD (56) exceed 8%.[107] The influence of previous coal mining activities on these proportions is unmistakable. There is a concentration of derelict spoil heaps in the western, northern and eastern parts of the conurbation with the central authorities and southern authorities relatively free of this type of land pollution. There appears to be no relationship between the acreages of derelict solid waste and current industrial activity as measured by individual industry or manufacturing industry employment statistics. This is not surprising in view of the period which has elapsed between the original generation of the waste and its present classification as derelict.

The main effect of derelict spoil heaps and derelict domestic and industrial tips in Greater Manchester is probably upon amenity. In addition, they obliterate wild-life and because of the nature of the wastes, 'poison' land for alternative uses by virtue, for example, of high heavy metal concentrations. They also contribute to water pollution since percolation waters and run-off sometimes contain acids, metals, or suspended solids. For example, a chemical waste tip in Bolton CB (1) gives rise to around 450 ppm of chromium in drainage waters severely reducing biota in the River Croal[125] (a current reclamation scheme should reduce this level considerably). Again, derelict spoil heaps and tips can contribute to air pollution by virtue of windblown dust (the formation of a surface shell of weathered vegetation and/or tipped material reduces this and other effects) and in the case of certain coal spoil heaps by internal 'heating'.[123]

Forecasting future quantities of derelict land depends upon two factors. The first is the rate of formation of derelict spoil heaps and tips. It is not possible to extrapolate time series based upon the doubtful official figures. On the whole, however, new derelict heaps and tips should be less numerous than has been the case in the past, since there is evidence that tighter planning conditions are beginning to have an effect on the after-treatment of both mineral spoil and waste tipping. Apart from this, the acreage of active spoil heaps and the acreages of refuse and industrial waste tips are also expected to fall. The second factor is the rate of reclamation of derelict land. Recontouring, deep ploughing and the application of a topsoil cover are often sufficient to sustain hardy grasses and some shrubs or trees, but toxicity or water-logging of some wastes necessitate careful drainage, neutralisation and the selection of resistant plants.[125] The grants to carry out this type of work have encouraged local planning authorities to initiate extensive programmes to reclaim derelict land. The 1150 acres of spoil heaps programmed over the next 6 or 7 years should ensure that 15–25% of existing spoil heaps and tips may be reclaimed by 1975 and perhaps 50–60% by 1981. As net new dereliction falls, the area of derelict spoil heaps and tips remaining in the Greater Manchester area by the latter year may be reduced to 2000 acres.

Litter

Litter consists of domestic and industrial wastes deposited outside the normal system of waste disposal. Apart from the usual small items of 'true' litter (litter dropped by the man in the street), market detritus, fly-tipping of both large domestic articles and vehicle loads of industrial waste generate 'gross' litter problems in Greater Manchester. Like derelict spoil heaps and tips, litter causes damage to amenity and until it is collected or absorbed into the environment it also, by definition, constitutes pollution.

Quantities of litter collected from streets and squares[103] and from public parks and green spaces[86] by local authorities in the conurbation vary considerably, reflecting both differing collection patterns and the considerable doubt which must be attached to estimated tonnages. The amounts removed from both types of area are highly correlated with resident population (and in the latter case with area of parkland), the relationships being very similar to that between refuse quantities and population, indicating the overwhelming importance of numbers of persons in explaining the generation of these types of wastes. Litter statistics could not, however, be related to the socio-economic characteristics of the various local authorities. In Greater Manchester as a whole around 60,000 tons of litter are collected by local authorities, of which probably less than 10,000 tons is true litter.[86, 103]

The effects of litter are similar to those of refuse disposal, although on a smaller and more diffuse scale. As in the case of refuse disposal, there have been a few cases of death of farm stock,[86] but the impact of litter upon aesthetic conditions—the most pervasive type of damage—could not be quantified.

Although little can be said of likely trends in industrial dumping, fly-tipping of domestic articles may well decrease in the future with the expected provision of better collection and disposal facilities for bulky items by local authorities.[131] On the other hand, the amount of ordinary (true) litter is expected to increase, mainly because of the trend towards disposable packaging and containers and the current lack of public concern about this pollution problem.

There is no single satisfactory measure of the effect of pollution from all the wastes discussed in this chapter. However, the proportion of a local authority's acreage occupied by active and derelict spoil heaps and tips provides some measure of the effect of many of the wastes. This information is summarised in Table 11.[107] Because of the difficulty in distinguishing between active and derelict sites and between mineral, domestic and industrial wastes, and because of the use of tips for more than one purpose, it is probably only by adding the areas used for all types of solid waste disposal within a local authority together to obtain total acreage of land occupied that an accurate assessment of these types of land pollution can be made.

The proportions of despoiled and derelict land vary from zero in a number of local authorities to 18% in the authority having the smallest area in Greater Manchester: Lees UD (45). The proportion also exceeds 10% in Swinton and Pendlebury MB (24) and Ince-in-Makerfield UD (42). In all, there are about 5500 acres of land occupied by solid waste in Greater Manchester, 1·5% of the total area. The proportions are also shown in Figure 21. There is no clear pattern to the distribution of land

pollution, but the higher proportions tend to occur in localities where
coal mining is or has been important. There are a number of southern
authorities where proportions are very low and, while this may to some
extent reflect differences in surveying procedures between local planning

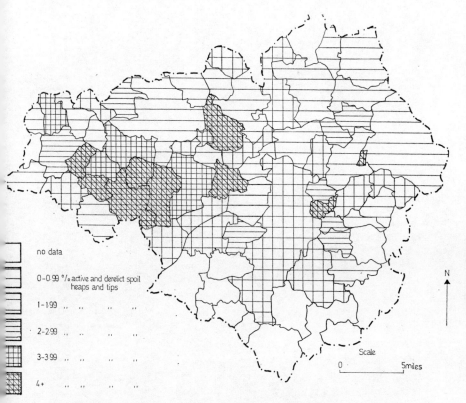

no data

0–0.99 % active and derelict spoil
        heaps and tips

1–1.99 „   „   „   „

2–2.99 „   „   „   „

3–3.99 „   „   „   „

4+   „   „   „   „

N

Scale

0   5miles

Figure 21   Proportions of local authorities occupied by active and
derelict spoil heaps and tips, 1972

authorities,[107] there does appear to be significantly less land pollution
in this part of the conurbation than in the remainder.

There is no significant statistical association between this measure
of land pollution and employment density, population density or car
ownership (Chapter 2). However, there is a positive although not highly

significant correlation with socio-economic grouping index (see Appendix) implying that the less affluent authorities have the higher proportions of land occupied by solid waste. Conversely, the more affluent authorities suffer least from this type of land pollution, as indicated by Figure 21.

5 Water pollution

The demand for drinking water in Greater Manchester is supplied almost exclusively by upland reservoirs situated outside the conurbation, little water being furnished by bore-holes to aquifers and abstractions from rivers. Domestic water supplies thus only impinge on the other parts of the water cycle in the area when they become waste and the pollution of drinking water is consequently not discussed in this chapter. The first part of the chapter analyses the volume and quality of aqueous wastes discharged into the river system of Greater Manchester in the year 1970/1, and the resulting water quality (pollution) and damage with which they were associated. To achieve comparability with the analyses in previous chapters, these data have been adapted to local authority boundaries wherever this has been possible. In the second part of the chapter, trends in river quality in the conurbation as a whole over the last decade and tentative forecasts of river quality for 1980 are examined.

Aqueous wastes, 1970/1
Wastes enter the river system as discharges from sewage works and direct from industrial premises, as storm overflows from sewers, as run-off from adjacent urban and rural land and as deposits from the atmosphere. The available data on water-borne wastes within Greater Manchester relate almost exclusively to the first two discharges although some statistics on the number of unsatisfactory storm overflows in the sub-region are also available.

In 1970/1 there were 69 discharges from sewage works serving a population of 200 or more which were operated by 47 local authorities well dispersed over the Greater Manchester area. The sizes of these discharges varied considerably—40 being less than 1 million gallons/day (mgd) while the largest was 67 mgd.[132] The largest works had substantial catchment areas centred upon the major concentrations of population, such as Manchester CB (3) and Bolton CB (1), and frequently also served certain of the outlying authorities.

More detailed 1969/70 information on 46 of the sewage works was obtained from questionnaires returned by sewage works managers.[118] Sewage was usually treated by a combination of primary methods—screening, grit removal and sedimentation—followed by treatment using biological filters or activated sludge. Only 8 works recorded any form of tertiary treatment. The disposal of the sludge removed from the sewage has been described in Chapter 4. The River Authorities sought to impose the Royal Commission standard of a maximum of 30 mg/l for bio-chemical oxygen demand (BOD) and of 20 mg/l for suspended solids on all discharges.[133] Only about one-third of the 69 discharges in the area achieved this standard on a regular basis. One of the main reasons for the unsatisfactory effluents of the remainder was that the dry weather flow influent frequently exceeded the works design capacity. At the time of the postal survey, 22 works had plans to increase their capacity or to alter their treatment methods.

Thirty-four of the 46 sewage works received industrial effluent from a wide variety of industries: most commonly from food and drink manu-facturers, textile trades, chemical and allied industries and engineering works. Altogether the industrial component of their influent created problems at 13 works, usually because of the large quantity of organic matter they contained.[118]

In addition to the industrial effluent treated at sewage works there were, in 1970/1, 173 direct discharges from industrial premises into those rivers within the Greater Manchester area under the jurisdiction of the Mersey and Weaver River Authority,[132] (Figure 4). The total volume of these effluents, together with 8 into canals, was 492 mgd compared with 187 mgd (domestic and industrial effluent) from the 69 sewage works discharges. However, 395 mgd of the total volume was from 12 major discharges of cooling water which were relatively unpolluted.

The sources and locations of these direct industrial discharges are summarised in Table 13. As in the case of the industrial effluent treated at sewage works, the effluents arise from a wide variety of industries—but most commonly from paper and board manufacture, electricity generation, textile manufacture and from the chemical industry. The location of the discharges reflects the siting of the industrial activities from which they originate (Chapter 2). Thus the discharges from paper manufacturers were mostly in the eastern part of the sub-region, par-ticularly affecting the Goyt and the Roch. Discharges from electricity generation mainly occurred in the south east part of the area, especially

Source	Ir-well	Roch	Manch-ester Ship Canal	Medlock	Mersey	Tame	Croal	Glaze	Irk	Canals	Goyt	Mill-ingford Brook	Total
Paper & Board	9	9	-	-	1	2	3	-	-	2	7	-	33
Electricity Generation	7	-	4	-	11	9	1	-	-	-	-	-	32
Textile Manufacture (cotton and man made)	4	6	1	-	1	3	6	-	2	1	-	-	24
Chemical and Allied Industries	1	4	3	-	4	-	-	2	2	2	-	-	18
Farming	-	-	-	16	-	-	-	-	-	-	-	-	16
Rubber Processing	-	2	1	1	-	1	-	-	1	2	-	-	8
General Manufacturing	2	1	1	-	-	-	-	-	-	3	-	-	7
Gas & Coke	-	-	2	4	-	-	-	-	-	-	-	-	6
Soap & Detergent	1	-	4	-	-	-	-	-	-	-	-	-	5
Petroleum Refining	-	-	4	-	-	-	-	-	-	-	-	-	4
Drainage from Disposal Tips	1	-	-	-	-	-	-	3	-	-	-	-	4
Plastic Manufacture	-	-	-	-	-	2	-	1	-	1	-	-	4
Textile (Wool) Manufacture	-	3	-	-	-	-	-	-	-	-	-	-	3
Coal Mining	-	-	-	-	-	-	-	2	-	-	-	1	3
Engineering	-	-	-	-	2	-	-	-	1	-	-	-	3
Effluent from Water Treatment	-	-	-	-	-	-	1	1	-	-	-	-	2
Iron and Steel	-	-	2	-	-	-	-	-	-	-	-	-	2
Drainage from Active Mines	1	-	-	-	-	-	-	-	-	-	-	1	2
Other	2	1	1	-	-	-	-	1	-	-	-	-	5
TOTAL	28	26	23	21	19	17	11	10	9	8	7	2	181

Table 13 Number of main discharges from various industrial sources into the rivers of Greater Manchester, 1970/1

affecting the Mersey and the Irwell. Textile works discharged effluents almost exclusively into the rivers in the northern part of the area, especially the Croal, Irwell and Spodden, whereas chemical works discharged largely into the lower Mersey and the Manchester Ship Canal. Other direct industrial discharges were mainly confined to the central part of the sub-region.

The consent conditions for industrial discharges varied considerably, and covered a wide range of parameters. Only 54% of the discharges were generally considered to be satisfactory by the River Authority but, since these included large volumes of cooling water, they represented 80% of the total volume of industrial effluent. Those exceeding consent

conditions usually failed to meet the suspended solid, BOD or per-
manganate value conditions.

Variation in wastes between local authorities

The available data on the volume and BOD load of effluents from sewage
works and direct industrial discharges [132] have been aggregated on a
local authority basis. The resulting statistics are necessarily only approximate but they do supply a useful indication of the magnitude of
aqueous waste disposals within the different local authority areas.

The differences in effluent volume and BOD loads between local
authorities have been examined using multiple regression analyses (see
Appendix). It has been hypothesised that the volume and load arising
within an authority are attributable to the size of the resident population
served by the sewage works of the local authority and to the level and
composition of industrial activity within its area. The latter have been
measured using Standard Industrial Classification employment data
(Chapter 2) to allow a crude comparison of the importance of the main
effluent generating industries—food, chemicals, metals, textiles, paper
and electricity—at local authority level.

Approximately 40% of the variance in total effluent volume between
local authority areas can be explained by differences in the size of the
population served by the authority's sewage works, which can differ
substantially from the size of the resident population of the local
authority, and by variations in employment in the paper and board
industry. Certain of the other industrial employment variables, notably
employment in the electricity industry, were correlated with effluent
volume but were not statistically significant in the multiple regression
analyses because of their correlation with the other variables
included.

Considerably greater success was achieved in explaining variations in
total BOD levels between local authorities. Nearly 60% of the variance
was explained by five variables: the size of the population served by the
local authority sewage works, and employment in chemicals, metals,
textiles and paper. The coefficients for the employment variables are
quite large, ranging between 1·9 lbs BOD/day/employee in metal manufacture to 0·4 lbs/day/employee in textiles. The coefficient for the population variable is much smaller ($-0·03$ lbs/day/capita). The sign of this
last variable probably results from two conflicting elements: influent
BOD increases as population size grows but there is a tendency for the

larger sewage works in the sample to remove a greater proportion of the BOD load before discharge to the river.

Major variations in effluent levels remain when the local authority effluent volume and BOD statistics have been standardised to take account of differences in area size (Figures 22 and 23). These variations

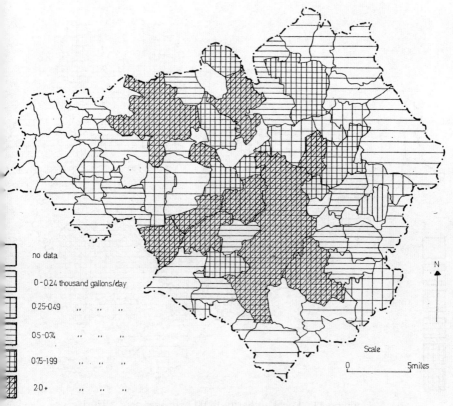

no data

0 - 0.24 thousand gallons/day

0.25-0.49   ,,   ,,   ,,

0.5-0.74   ,,   ,,   ,,

0.75-1.99   ,,   ,,   ,,

2.0+   ,,   ,,   ,,

N

Scale

0   5 miles

Figure 22   Local authority effluent volumes per acre, 1970/1

reflect differences in population density, in the level and composition of industrial activity and in the import and export of wastes for treatment between local authorities. The mainly central areas recording the highest values for effluent volume and BOD load also record high values for many of these waste generating variables. Areas with low waste levels

generally have fairly low population density and industrial activity
values and/or often export wastes for treatment in other areas.

In addition to these regular effluent discharges to the river system,
there were 544 unsatisfactory storm overflows in the Greater Manchester area.[132] This remarkably high number included 268 overflows

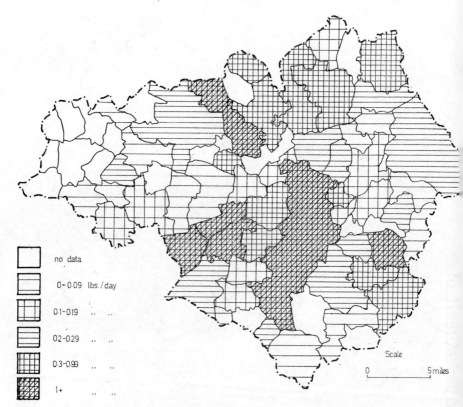

no data

0-0.09 lbs./day

0.1-0.19 ,,   ,,

0.2-0.29 ,,   ,,

0.3-0.99 ,,   ,,

1+   ,,   ,,

Scale

0   5 miles

Figure 23   Local authority BOD loads per acre, 1970/1

into the rivers Medlock and Irk, and their principal tributaries, which
run through the central authorities of Manchester CB (3), Oldham
CB (4), Middleton MB (17), Chadderton UD (32), Droylsden UD (36)
and Failsworth UD (37). The remainder of the unsatisfactory storm
overflows were fairly evenly distributed over the area.

No data are available on the importance or spatial distribution of contaminants from run-off into the river system. The extent of agricultural activity tends to be inversely related to population and industrial density (Chapter 2) but it does not necessarily mean that pollution caused by agricultural run-off follows the same pattern. Since agricultural practice becomes more intensive in areas of high population and/or industrial density, there is a consequent rise in animal wastes per agricultural area and this latter measure may be a more appropriate indication of certain types of run-off problem (see Chapter 4). In this case, the main location of both unsatisfactory storm overflows and run-off problems may be in areas with high effluent volume and BOD per acre ratios.

River quality, 1970

For the purposes of a recent national survey of river pollution, four-fold chemical and biological classifications of river quality were used.[134] The chemical classification was based almost wholly on BOD and dissolved oxygen levels with some qualitative assessment of other contaminants present and is referred to as Class 1: unpolluted; Class 2: doubtful; Class 3: poor; and Class 4: grossly polluted. The biological classification was based upon a number of biological indicators, including the ability to support different species of fish. The two classification systems did not coincide for all stretches of river but, when grouped on a local authority basis within the Greater Manchester area, the correlation between them was high ($r = 0.8$, $\alpha = 0.0005$). The biological index tends to indicate lower quality than the chemical index, partly because of fish kills due to episodic pollution by silage liquors, oil and chemicals (some of which is caused by road tanker accidents).[12] The chemical classification system has been used in this chapter but, given coincidence between the two systems, it can be assumed that Class 1 rivers will normally support game-fishing, that Class 2 rivers will normally support mixed coarse fisheries and that Class 4 rivers are incapable of supporting fish life.[134]

In 1970, of the 459 river miles within Greater Manchester, 153 miles fell into Class 1, and 114 miles into Class 2. It is therefore estimated that 58% of the total river length was capable of supporting at least mixed coarse fisheries. This, however, was well below the average of 91% for the whole of England and Wales. Of the remainder of the river system 78 miles (17%) were in Class 3 while 114 miles (25%) were of Class 4 quality.

The highest river quality was found in the upper reaches of rivers, away from the more densely populated and heavily industrialised areas of the sub-region. Both the Bollin and Millingford Brook (in the southwest of the area) were either Class 1 or Class 2 for their whole length. The uppermost reaches of the Tame and some of the tributaries of the Roch were also of Class 1 quality. In contrast, the worst quality was recorded for considerable stretches of the main rivers—the Roch itself, the Irwell, the Irk, the Medlock, the lower part of the Tame and the Manchester Ship Canal—running through the most densely populated and heavily industrialised part of the conurbation. A considerable polluting load is, in fact, exported from Greater Manchester by the Manchester Ship Canal. However, the input of wastes to the Canal and the Mersey outside the sub-region is such that the removal of its pollution would not raise the quality of the lower reaches of the river above Class 3.[12]

Variation in river quality between local authorities
The data on the chemical classification of the river system, by stretch, within Greater Manchester was used to construct an average water quality index for each constituent local authority area. This was obtained by calculating the total mileage of river in each of the four qualities in each local authority and then using these as weights in deriving a mean water quality for the authority area as a whole. For example, in Tyldesley UD (56) there were 1·2 miles in Class 1, 0·6 miles in Class 2, 0·9 miles in Class 3 and 3·0 miles in Class 4. The average water quality for this local authority was therefore 3·0 ((1·2+1·2+2·7+12·0)/5·7). The results of this exercise have been reproduced in Figure 24, which demonstrates that the worst river quality was to be found in the central part of the conurbation, notably to the east, north and west of Manchester CB (3). By contrast, with the exception of the area around Wigan CB (8), the outlying areas of the conurbation, especially to the south and the north east, have good or very good river quality.

Relationship between wastes and river quality
The quality of a river stretch is a function of the quality of the water in the preceding stretch, the pollution load discharged into the stretch, its dilution and the length of the stretch. The influence of two of these factors (BOD load discharged and length of stretch) on river quality is illustrated in Figure 25, using data for a sample of stretches within Greater Manchester. A similar kind of relationship can be obtained by

plotting BOD load against the flow of the stretch. On a local authority basis, the average water quality index should be a function of the mean water quality of the rivers at the point where they enter the authority and of the BOD load per mile of river within the local authority.

However, the process of averaging data on a local authority basis,

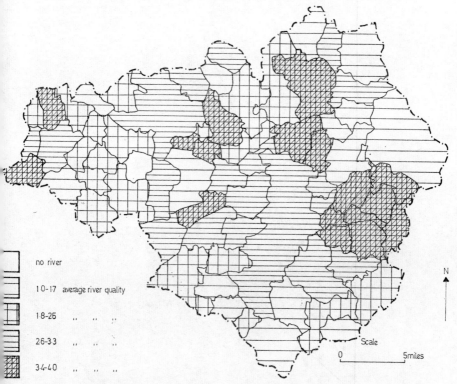

no river

1·0–1·7 average river quality

1·8–2·5 „   „   „

2·6–3·3 „   „   „

3·4–4·0 „   „   „

Figure 24 Local authority average river qualities, 1970

coupled with the neglect of river stretch lengths and flow, precludes the explanation of a high proportion of the variation in average river quality between local authorities. Nevertheless, both these explanatory variables are shown to be statistically significant and to have the expected positive correlation with the average river quality index. The coefficient for the inflowing water quality variable is less than one, as would be expected given the partial self-purification of the polluted inflowing water as it flows through the local authority area (see Appendix).

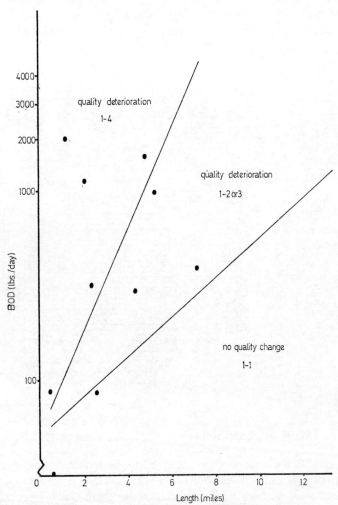

Figure 25   Relationship between BOD and length of river
stretch in Greater Manchester, initial quality Class 1

Socio-economic significance of variations in river quality
The variations in average river quality between local authorities have been explained principally in terms of differences in the quality of their inflowing river water and, because of their relationship with BOD load, differences in population density and in industrial structure. In fact, a regression between average river quality and population density showed the expected close relationship ($r=0.31$, $\alpha=0.001$). It is also desirable to establish the relationship between the socio-economic characteristics of local authorities and river pollution. These characteristics, as stated in Chapter 2, have been measured in terms of a socio-economic grouping index which is closely inversely correlated with both income and car ownership levels.

Within the Greater Manchester sub-region as a whole there was a general tendency for river quality to be best in those areas with the lowest SEG index (i.e. with the highest incomes) and worst in the areas at the opposite end of the socio-economic scale. This is reflected in regression analyses which indicate a positive, though not strong, linear relationship between socio-economic grouping index and average river quality ($r=0.22$, $\alpha=0.05$) and a negative correlation between car ownership and average river quality ($r=-0.42$, $\alpha=0.05$) in the various local authorities within the sub-region.

As previously indicated in Chapter 2, there would appear to be two types of low income (high socio-economic grouping index) local authority areas in Greater Manchester. One type is fairly centrally located within the conurbation and generally has poor river quality. The second type is mainly found in the north and west of the area near its perimeter, and tends to have much better river quality. If it were not for this second type of authority, the positive correlation between socio-economic grouping index and river quality would be much higher.

The central low income local authority areas display a number of characteristics which are associated with high effluent volumes and BOD loads per acre and per river mile. Firstly, they tend to have high population densities. Secondly, these same areas have fairly high industrial employment densities. Thirdly, there is evidence that the larger sewage works, located in the lower income authorities of the sub-region, are receiving effluent from certain types of the more prosperous suburban and outlying areas.[132] It is these waste-generating characteristics, combined with the tendency for their inflowing river water to be of low quality, which explain why river quality is least satisfactory in these low income areas. The policy significance of this situation is examined in Chapter 7.

Pollution of canals and enclosed waters, 1970
Within the Greater Manchester area, canals and enclosed waters provide alternative sources of water supply and amenity to the river system.

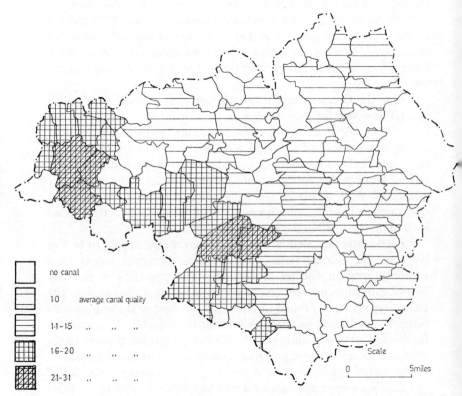

no canal

1·0   average canal quality

1·1 – 1·5   „   „   „

1·6 – 2·0   „   „   „

2·1 – 3·1   „   „   „

Scale

0   5 miles

Figure 26 Local authority average canal qualities, 1970

It was therefore necessary to consider how far the conclusions reached above should be modified when the quality of these alternative sources were taken into account.

The canal system was included in the national river survey,[134] stretches being classified by the same chemical criteria as rivers. It is notable that the canal system (excluding the Manchester Ship Canal) within Greater

Manchester was apparently of considerably better quality than the river system.[12, 134] Of the total of 101 miles of canal, 60% were of Class 1 quality, 32·5% Class 2, 1·5% Class 3, and 6% Class 4 (Figure 26).

Whilst the facilities of Class 1 canals and rivers are not identical and, in any case, the canal system is considerably less extensive than the river system, these canals nevertheless provide an important additional source of supply for water-related activities. Furthermore, although some of the poorest quality canal water is to be found in a few local authority areas with poor river quality, in general the reverse is true, since the correlation with river quality is inverse ($r = -0·31$, $\alpha = 0·025$). Therefore, it would seem that many of the more central, low income areas are gaining some partial compensation for their poor river quality. Similarly, although the information is more sparse, it would appear that pollution incidents affecting enclosed waters are not correlated with average river quality in local authority areas.[86]

Waste trends

Because of limitations in data, BOD has been used as a proxy for all wastes when examining the trend in the waste loading of the river system. Although this is widely accepted as a general indicator, it does not necessarily reflect the trend in other waste parameters, e.g. phosphates, nitrates, detergents, pesticides or metals. For similar reasons, the data used refer only to the Mersey and Weaver River Authority section of the area and are limited to the years 1966–71 inclusive.

Table 14 indicates the trends in BOD levels into the individual rivers within Greater Manchester and into their upper reaches prior to entering the area.[132] Between 1966/7 and 1970/1 the combined load fell, although not steadily, from 300,000 lbs/day to 250,000 lbs/day. However, although the loading into the upper reaches of the rivers rising outside the conurbation (the Bollin, Etherow, Goyt and Irwell) fell by 68%, total loading within the sub-region itself only fell by 16%. In part, this reflects the River Authority's apparent policy of initiating improvements at the sources of rivers.

Within Greater Manchester there were important changes in BOD load distribution, even over this short period. The BOD load of the Manchester Ship Canal nearly doubled over this period, but, apart from an increase in the very small load of Millingford Brook, BOD discharges into other rivers fell by varying degrees. This situation again reflects the short-term procedure of the River Authority in using the

	1966/67	1967/68	1968/69	1969/70	1970/71
Bollin - within GMA	500	700	800	600	600
- outside GMA	4,000	4,800	1,500	1,700	1,800
Croal	14,600	17,000	13,500	12,000	7,400
Etherow - within GMA	400	500	400	300	400
- outside GMA	4,500	3,400	2,400	2,400	2,100
Glaze	3,800	3,100	3,000	3,200	3,200
Goyt - within GMA	6,500	5,100	5,100	4,700	5,000
- outside GMA	12,400	9,200	7,300	6,600	3,400
Irk	10,400	8,300	7,500	8,000	2,500
Irwell - within GMA	54,000	23,200	20,600	19,700	16,600
-outside GMA	16,000	12,700	6,200	5,600	4,600
Manchester Ship Canal	64,500	79,200	112,100	102,600	126,500
Mersey	60,800	56,800	65,800	67,400	42,000
Millingford Brook	300	300	400	400	400
Medlock	4,100	4,300	4,200	1,500	1,300
Roch	21,000	17,400	19,700	20,100	18,900
Tame	22,900	35,100	21,600	16,600	16,700
Total loading within Greater Manchester	263,800	250,800	274,700	257,200	241,600
Total loading into upper reaches of rivers flowing into Greater Manchester	36,900	30,100	17,400	16,400	11,900
TOTAL LOADING	300,700	281,000	292,000	273,500	253,500

N.B.   Totals do not agree because of rounding.

Table 14   BOD loading of discharges into the rivers of
Greater Manchester, 1966/7–1970/1 (lbs/day)

Manchester Ship Canal as a major effluent disposal channel for the sub-region.

Reduction in total load has been due both to a drop in the number of discharges and to an improvement in the quality of those remaining. During this period, discharges from seven sewage works and 50 important industrial discharges were discontinued. Partially offsetting this effect was the introduction of 12 new industrial discharges.

Industrial discharges have been terminated for two reasons: closure of premises (relatively common in the area with the closing of textile works) or diversion of effluents to a sewage works.[12] The latter results not only in a geographic redistribution of, but often also a reduction in, the polluting load because the treatment facilities used have usually been more efficient than those they have replaced. Thus, on average, the BOD load (in mg/l) for discontinued discharges in their final year of operation was 93 for sewage works and 2852 for industrial works. By comparison, the corresponding averages for all works still in operation in 1970/1 was 38 (sewage works) and 225 (industrial premises).

Among those discharges that remain, the trend in BOD load has not been uniform. Fifty-eight major discharges increased their load whilst 87 either remained the same or were reduced. Where reductions were achieved, they were accomplished by improved effluent quality or reduction in effluent volume.[132]

River quality trends

The Mersey and Weaver River Authority provided, for the purpose of this study, the results of their chemical analyses of river quality within Greater Manchester. From these it was possible to examine the changes in river quality at 41 points within the area by applying a four-grade scale, similar to that used in the national river survey, for each quarter 1958–70. These data were then used to assess the general trend in river quality in Greater Manchester as a whole and in each of its main rivers.

A single water quality score for the entire area was derived by adding the number of points falling into each water quality class for each quarter, then multiplying this sum by the value of the class, adding the results for the four quarters, and finally finding the mean value for the 41 points, which could range from 1·0 to 4·0. More sophisticated measures which took account of the length of stretch or flow of water appropriate to each monitoring point did not materially affect the trends obtained and therefore have not been reported.

The results obtained (Figure 27) are partly influenced by the variations in annual rainfall which affect the dilution of pollutants in the river system. After these variations have been taken into account, a clearly favourable time trend in river quality remains, with the water quality score improving, on average, by 0·05 points per annum. During the period 1958/9 to 1964/5, the improvement was very slight, but between 1964/5 and 1967/8 it became more pronounced, and then quality became relatively stable until 1970. The time series data for BOD loading only relate to 1966–71 (Table 14) but it is apparent that river quality during this period largely mirrored the trends occurring in the BOD of discharges.

The trends in BOD loadings and chemical classification are by no means uniform in all the Greater Manchester rivers. Three groups of rivers may be distinguished. The first consists of rivers which showed a significant improvement in quality, especially during the second half of the 1960s and included the rivers Irwell, Croal, Etherow and Goyt. In all of these cases there was a significant reduction in BOD loadings, especially in their upper reaches. The second group consists of rivers

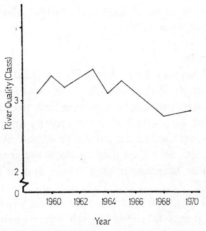

Figure 27   Greater Manchester river qualities,
1958–70

that showed no significant improvement before 1970. Chief among these are the Manchester Ship Canal, Millingford Brook, the Mersey, Glaze and Irk which did not benefit from a reduction in BOD loading during the 1966/9 period. Finally, there was a small miscellaneous group including the Roch (which improved dramatically in the early 1960s, but in line with the trend in its BOD load did not change afterwards), and the Medlock and the Tame (which changed little during this period but were beginning to improve towards the end as BOD levels fell). In general, water quality in the central densely populated and industrialised authorities, through which the fairly mature rivers flow, has changed relatively little in the last decade.

Limited observations on nitrate, phosphate and synthetic detergent levels in the river system were available for the latter half of the 1960s. In most of the rivers nitrate levels and, to a lesser degree, phosphate levels were rising whilst synthetic detergent concentrations were generally stationary or falling. In all three cases the absolute levels recorded were fairly low relative to those where significant damage is to be expected. Data on metal and pesticide concentrations in river water are insufficient to establish trends in these pollutants.

Forecasts

Given the quality of the data available and the complexity of the river quality trends over the past decade, only the most general indication of likely future trends can be given. As in the case of other types of waste disposal, it is desirable to know the likely pattern of future land use in each of the local authority areas, identifying particularly changes in population density and industrial structure. However, the situation will also be affected by changes in the level of waste treatment and the extent to which this occurs will depend upon the policy decisions of the new regional water authority.

For the purpose of the national river survey the River Authority noted 'those sections of the watercourse which could be expected to be upgraded following remedial action on those discharges which are at present unsatisfactory'.[135] If all such work were completed by 1980 and, if no major new source of river deterioration were to emerge, then the changes in river quality shown in Table 15 would be expected.[132]

Year	Class 1	Class 2	Class 3	Class 4
1970	153	114	78	114
1980	168	181	97	14

Table 15 River quality in the rivers of Greater Manchester administered by the Mersey and Weaver River Authority, 1970 and, assuming remedial works are completed, 1980 (miles)

When these 1980 data are converted into the previously described water quality score, then the index is forecast to fall from 2·8 (1969/70) to 2·3. It has already been established that the water quality score is falling (by 0·05 points per annum between 1958–70) and if this trend were to continue then the projected score of 2·3 would be reached in 1978/9.

The changes envisaged by 1980 imply a substantial upgrading of Class 3 and Class 4 river water to Class 2 or Class 3, respectively. In biological terms this would mean a substantial increase in the river mileage where good mixed coarse fishing could take place, with consequent increase in amenity values. Also, it is likely that a proportion of these improvements will occur in some of those low income areas which experienced little improvement in river quality during the last decade.

Whilst these projected improvements are very considerable, there are two senses in which the 1980 situation may still be judged unsatisfactory. The expected proportion of rivers in Greater Manchester in 1980 which will be of Class 1 and 2 quality will still be below the 1970 national average.[134] It also appears probable that the poor quality river stretches which remain will continue to be mainly concentrated in the more centrally located, less affluent parts of the conurbation.

6 Noise pollution

A further important waste which may lead to environmental pollution is surplus energy in the form of noise from industrial, traffic and domestic sources. Whilst, at the levels which normally prevail in the environment, this may not be a physical hazard to hearing,[2] it is a pervasive and increasing source of annoyance, especially in urban and suburban residential areas and the resulting stress may, in certain circumstances, adversely affect mental health.[136]

Unfortunately, data on both noise emissions and environmental levels in Greater Manchester are deficient. There has been no comprehensive monitoring survey comparable to that previously undertaken in London.[137, 138] It would appear that only a minority of the local authorities in the conurbation regularly take noise measurements and these are mainly linked to investigations by public health inspectors concerning specific noise complaints. Given these data limitations, the structure of this chapter differs from that of those immediately preceding it. The first section contains a general review of noise problems within Greater Manchester, using mainly the information obtained from postal questionnaires returned by Chief Public Health Inspectors.[53] The second section consists of a more detailed examination of road and air traffic noise. The final section of the chapter summarises the geographical distribution of noise problems and expected future trends in the conurbation.

General review of noise problems in Greater Manchester
In the absence of satisfactory noise monitoring data, the best general sources of information about noise annoyance are the public health departments of the constituent local authorities. These possess certain statutory powers in relation to noise nuisances from industrial, commercial, construction, entertainment and domestic sources but not from road traffic or aircraft.[35] The Chief Public Health Inspectors of each local authority were asked to indicate any major and persistent sources of noise within their area, as part of the postal surveys described in Chapter 2.[53] Of the 59 who responded, 28 specifically mentioned in-

dustrial sources, 21 road traffic, 5 building and road construction, 9 domestic, neighbourhood and entertainment sources and 4 aircraft noise.

Since noise is dissipated within a relatively small distance of its source, it is to be expected that the incidence of noise problems will be correlated with the industrial, traffic and population densities of the local authorities in which they occur. This is largely confirmed by the available evidence. Of the 26 local authorities whose industrial employment per acre ratio exceeds 2·0 (Table 3, Figure 7) 20 specifically mention industrial noise as a major problem. Similarly, seven of the ten authorities with the highest traffic densities (see next section) claimed to have major road traffic noise problems whereas only two of the 21 authorities reporting this kind of noise problem had traffic densities lower than the median authority.

The much more geographically restricted problem of major or persistent aircraft noise was experienced in local authorities adjacent to the main airport in the conurbation (Ringway) and, to a lesser extent, in those adjacent to smaller aircraft testing sites. Neighbourhood and entertainment noise are much more diffuse and less easily explained phenomena. Nevertheless, problems of these types were mainly associated with the older, medium density towns in the sub-region where entertainment and residential land uses are only partially segregated.

Complaints data and noise trends
This information on noise problems can be supplemented by an analysis of noise complaint statistics, also gathered in the postal survey, for the same 59 authorities.[53] However, such data are really unsuitable both for identifying the major noise problems in the sub-region and for identifying the particular areas where noise problems are most severe. In general, the annual number of recorded noise complaints relative to population size is so small (ranging between 0·2 and 13·0/10,000 population) that the actions of a very small minority can have a disproportionate effect on complaint statistics. Also, the data may be biased because complaints are made less frequently by lower income groups[137] and are seldom about noise problems (e.g. road traffic noise)[53] for which Public Health Inspectors possess very limited powers of action. One authority, for example, which is amongst the most heavily industrialised, densely populated and vehicle trafficked within the sub-region, was found to have the lowest noise complaints per population ratio among all the authorities for which complaint statistics were available.

However, time series data on complaints within individual authorities, may perhaps be more justifiably used to assess trends in particular kinds of noise problem within the sub-region. Table 16 summarises the in-

Source	Increase	No Change	Decrease	No reply
Industry	23	16	10	10
Domestic	9	28	2	20
Road Traffic	11	28	0	20
Aircraft	5	27	0	25

Table 16 Trends in noise complaints to local authority public health departments in Greater Manchester, 1967–72 (numbers of authorities)

formation supplied by Chief Public Health Inspectors. It indicates that, in relation to each of the four main noise sources, the volume of complaints is rising over time, although this does not apply to industrial noise complaints in a minority of local authorities.

The rise in the total volume of noise complaints within Greater Manchester reflects the national trend in which noise complaints to the Public Health Inspectorate are increasing by as much as 10% per annum.[139] An obvious possible cause of this increase is that ambient noise levels are becoming higher, but there may be two additional factors influencing the situation. Evidence already exists[137] that sensitivity to noise is greater amongst the higher socio-economic groups, so that noise annoyance may be increasing, independently of any change in noise levels, as real incomes rise. Secondly, with the emergence of environmental pressure groups, greater environmental awareness and public participation in local authority affairs, the propensity to make complaints to public health departments may be increasing.

Data on trends in ambient noise levels attributable to industrial sources and the annoyance they cause in Greater Manchester are not available but, according to the Chief Inspector of Factories, there is no doubt that these are rising in the country as a whole. 'A very small amount of energy released as sound can cause a great deal of noise, and with the steadily increasing levels of energy per head of population, and industry always tending to achieve greater production in the same space and time, it is hardly surprising that industry tends to become noisier as the years go by.'[140]

In the same report the Chief Inspector refers to the results of a small survey of noise levels in industry. A feature of the results is the frequency with which high noise levels were reported in metals manufacture, engineering and textile factories.[140] Two of these three industries are well represented in Greater Manchester and, where Public Health Inspectors have indicated the type of industrial noise that causes major or persistent problems, these three industries are the most frequently mentioned. The decline in the traditional textile industry may be a partial cause of the decrease in industrial noise complaints in certain of the cotton towns (Table 16). However, this is not a general pattern since the conversion of old mills to other uses, such as plastics processing, can give rise to new noise problems.

Data on countrywide trends in noise levels attributable to domestic sources are not available but fairly conclusive evidence of a rising trend due to increased road and air traffic noise emissions does exist. During the last decade the total vehicle mileage on British roads has virtually doubled.[15] This has been mainly due to the sharp increase in the level of car ownership, although the number of goods vehicles, especially of the larger type, has also increased considerably. Since the average noise emission from the individual vehicle has not declined, the noise climate attributable to motor vehicle traffic has consequently risen appreciably. By 1970, it was estimated that 'between 19% and 46% of the UK urban population of 45m live in roads with traffic flows which produce noise levels likely to be judged undesirable for residential areas'.[141] These estimates do not take into account the further noise annoyance due to the increased need for road construction and repair work which accounted for approximately 20% of all confirmed noise nuisances in 1971.[139] Air travel, increasing at annual rates in excess of 10%,[15] has grown even more dramatically than road traffic. The number and size of aeroplanes have risen to cope with this demand for air travel, causing sharply increasing noise levels below flight paths adjacent to major airports. The noise levels attributable to road and air traffic in the Greater Manchester area are examined further in the next section.

Road traffic noise
Estimates of the volume of peak hour road traffic in 1966 for each link within the main road system of the SELNEC area are available from the SALTS Transportation Study.[34] Since traffic volume is one of the major determinants of the level of road traffic noise these data were used as a basis for assessing the difference in road traffic noise levels as well as

vehicular air pollution between districts (Chapters 2 and 3). Before outlining the ways in which the data were used and the results obtained, it is necessary to refer briefly to certain limitations in the traffic data.

In addition to the errors in traffic estimates for certain individual road links and the systematic understatement of total vehicle miles in all districts mentioned in Chapter 2, all the traffic volume data are in the form of passenger car equivalents (pcu's) which imply a uniform traffic mix between cars and lorries. On routes where heavy goods vehicle traffic is more prominent (in industrial areas or on routes between such areas) the relative magnitude of road traffic noise may be understated. Similarly, the available traffic data do not contain information on road gradients, vehicle speeds or the flow characteristics of the traffic, all of which can influence the noise environment. Most important of all, there is no parallel inventory of roadside conditions available which permits a calculation of the proportions of the resident population at different distances from the kerbside on each link.

Given the type of data available it was decided to make two types of road traffic noise comparison between districts within the SELNEC area—one based upon road link data and the second upon total traffic volumes within districts. In each case, the deficiencies mentioned above must be borne in mind.

Road link traffic
Using the formula developed by Scholes and Sargent[142] the traffic volumes on individual road links have been classified according to their expected noise level range. These ranges (Table 17) have been calculated

Link Loading (peak period pcu's)	< 500	500-1000	1000-2000	2000+
Noise range Equivalent (dB (A))	< 68	68- 70.5	70.5 - 73	73+

Table 17 Estimated noise levels from various road link traffic volumes

assuming a distance of 30 metres from the kerbside, that 20% of traffic is composed of goods vehicles and that any noise reduction due to lower speeds is offset by a noise increase because of the absence of free flow conditions.

Previous studies [2, 137] have indicated that peak noise and variations in noise may be more significant in explaining annoyance than average noise levels. A number of measures have been developed which take these considerations into account of which the simplest (the L_{10} unit) measures the peak noise level which is exceeded for 10% of the daily period, 6.00 a.m. to midnight. Since the traffic volume data relate to peak loadings, their noise equivalent must approximately correspond to this L_{10} measure. A number of investigations [2] have also shown that where L_{10} levels exceed 65–70 dB(A) the noise causes sufficient annoyance to be regarded as undesirable in residential areas.

It is conservatively assumed in this study that the L_{10} level is exceeded where the peak pcu flow is greater than 1000. Table 4 indicates that several SELNEC districts are apparently experiencing these peak traffic volumes on a significant proportion of their main road networks, especially in the more central areas of the conurbation. Peak traffic volumes in excess of 2000 pcu's (73 dB(A)) were found on 40% of total link length in four districts to the northwest of central Manchester and on over 20% of the total link length in several districts to the immediate west, south and east of the central business district. Altogether, over 50 districts had peak traffic volumes greater than 1000 pcu's on at least 20% of their main road network. Therefore, it would appear that only a small number of districts, chiefly located on the outskirts of the conurbation, do not have a significant noise problem in the vicinity of their main roads.

Average traffic volumes
The traffic data relating to road links cannot be used to compare traffic noise levels between districts unless the total main road mileage and the area of each district are also taken into account. When these are considered the ranking of districts is similar to that obtained using a much simpler measure, pcu miles per square mile, in each district.

The traffic density of districts within the SELNEC area, as measured by pcu miles per square mile, have been shown in Table 4 and Figure 9. On this basis, the highest noise levels occur in central Manchester and in central Stockport. The next highest levels occur in districts of two kinds—districts immediately surrounding central Manchester and the central parts of the county boroughs in the northern part of the conurbation. The third highest category includes districts mainly located to the immediate north and east and, more extensively, to the south and west of the districts immediately around central Manchester. Districts estimated to have the lowest average noise levels are to be found in the outer areas of the conurbation, notably to the extreme north and south.

The extent of the annoyance caused by these different levels of traffic noise will partially depend upon the residential population densities in the districts to which they apply. In the central areas of Manchester and the nearby towns, for example, although noise levels may be high, average residential population densities are fairly low. If the traffic density measure is weighted by the population density in each district, then it is the more densely populated areas immediately surrounding central Manchester which appear in the highest noise annoyance categories. Conversely, the lower population densities in the outlying areas of the conurbation reinforce their low traffic densities in causing low annoyance.

These conclusions on the noise ranking of districts take no account of inter-district variations in local traffic. The extent of local commercial traffic is likely to depend upon the amount of commercial and industrial activity in the district and could therefore mirror the incidence of in-dustrial noise problems discussed earlier in this chapter. The intensity of local car traffic is likely to vary between districts according to the level of car ownership/square mile. Since the high per capita car owner-ship rates of the more affluent districts are partially offset by lower population densities, car ownership/square mile is highest in the districts to the immediate south of Manchester Central—Manchester South, South Central and West and Sale (Figure 28). In both instances, therefore, it seems unlikely that the pattern of local traffic will greatly modify the main conclusions already reached on inter-area differences in noise levels within Greater Manchester.

Air traffic noise
Although aircraft noise is a more restricted problem than other forms of noise in its geographical extent, it is the most significant source of noise annoyance within a limited number of local authorities. Whilst a small number of local authority areas are affected by aeroplane testing opera-tions and one authority, apparently, by helicopter operations,[53] the main areas affected are under the flight paths from the international airport at Ringway (in Bucklow RD (70)). This airport is currently the third largest in the country and its growth has more than kept pace with the very rapid increase in air travel during the last decade.[143]

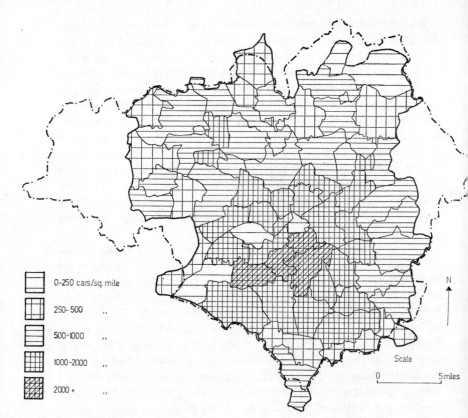

0-250 cars/sq. mile	
250-500 ,,	
500-1000 ,,	
1000-2000 ,,	
2000+ ,,	

Figure 28   SELNEC district car ownership densities, 1966

Noise annoyance from aircraft is measured in this country according to the Noise and Number Index (NNI).[2] This Index takes account both of the peak noise level of the individual aircraft and the total number of aircraft movements. Using a survey commissioned by Manchester Corporation it has been possible to estimate the daytime NNI contours for 1970 in relation to the boundaries of the local authorities mainly affected[144] (Figure 29).

Aircraft noise during the day in the 40-50 NNI range becomes in-trusive or annoying in residential areas and maximum 'acceptable' levels probably lie within the range 50-60 NNI.[2,143] Therefore it would seem that daytime noise levels were very annoying in parts of four local authorities, Cheadle and Gatley UD (33), Manchester CB (3), Wilmslow

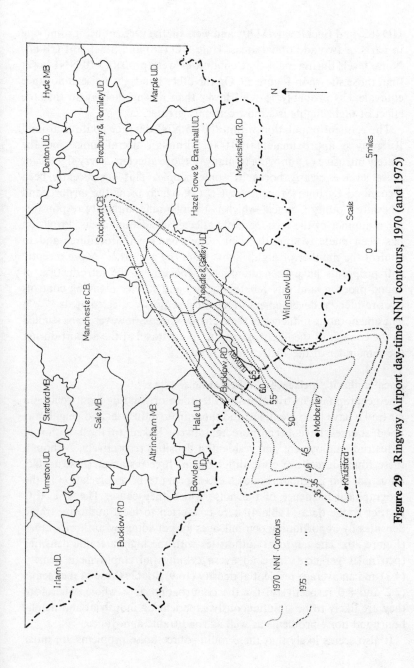

Figure 29 Ringway Airport day-time NNI contours, 1970 (and 1975)

UD (62) and Bucklow RD (70), and were on the verge of being annoying in parts of two additional areas, Hale UD (38) and Stockport CB (7). Noise levels during night-time conditions were probably 10 NNI lower than those shown in Figure 29. On the other hand, the noise annoyance equivalent is probably 15 NNI lower than during the day so that the effect of night flights is almost certainly greater.

The resident population within the 35 NNI daytime contour around Ringway is approximately 100,000. Although aircraft noise may be merely intrusive or annoying to many of those affected, a very significant noise level is clearly borne by some people. This has recently been recognised by both Manchester CB (3), which owns the airport, and Cheshire County Council, which is the planning authority responsible for a number of the most severely affected residential areas. Provision has been made to apply special noise abatement procedures and to control the number of night flights from the airport.[144] More recently still proposals have been announced concerning the introduction of sound-proofing and rate rebate schemes and stricter planning controls over residential development in the most seriously affected areas.[145-147] The ameliorating influence of these changes needs, however, to be studied in the context of the likely expansion in air travel at the airport during the remainder of the 1970s and beyond.

Local authority incidence of different noise types

The geographical distributions of the noise originating from road and air traffic have been identified and those from industrial and neighbourhood sources have been more tentatively linked to local authority industrial employment and residential densities respectively. Although these four sources are quite different, in three instances (road traffic, industrial and neighbourhood) there appears to be a correlation in the geographical incidence of the noise which they cause. The SELNEC district traffic data (Table 4) were converted to local authority traffic densities by apportioning pcu mileages and dividing by authority areas (Figure 30). The ten local authorities with the highest traffic densities (pcu miles per acre) have an average industrial employment density (4·7) and an average residential density (16·9) double those of the means (2·2 and 8·0 respectively) for the conurbation as a whole. Therefore they are likely to be simultaneously experiencing industrial and neighbourhood noise problems as well as road traffic annoyance.

It also seems likely that these multi-source noise problems are most acute in a certain type of low income area. This conclusion is based upon the positive correlation already established between the socio-economic grouping index, car ownership and income of local authorities and pcu miles per square mile, industrial density and residential density (Chapters 2 and 3). These areas are mainly to be found around the centre of

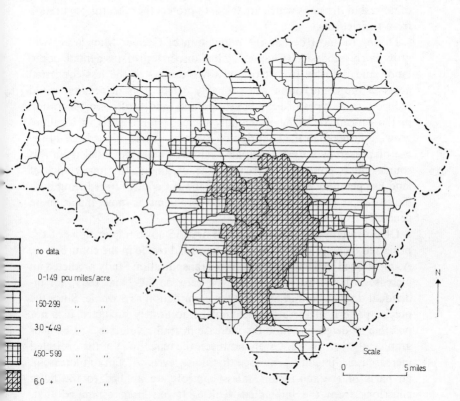

no data

0-1·49 pcu miles/acre

1·50-2·99 ,, ,,

3·0 -4·49 ,, ,,

4·50-5·99 ,, ,,

6·0 + ,, ,,

N

Scale

0   5 miles

Figure 30 Local authority peak period traffic densities, 1966

the conurbation and in certain of its nearby towns, especially in the north. By contrast, in the high income areas located in the outer southern parts of the conurbation, traffic volumes and residential densities are much lower and industrialisation is minimal. The distribution of aircraft noise does not closely correlate with any of the above variables and the authorities affected by this type of noise vary considerably in

income level, although the most severely affected locality is a low income housing estate (within Manchester CB (3)).

Forecasts

Future noise levels and the annoyance they cause within Greater Manchester will greatly depend upon changes in the four major determinants
of noise and the steps which are taken to protect the receptor population
from their effects.

During the next decade the population of Greater Manchester will
grow fairly modestly (Chapter 2) but dispersion of residential population and industry from city and town centres to the less congested
areas of the conurbation will probably occur. This dispersion would
reduce certain types of neighbourhood and industrial noise generation
in the central areas but potentially increase noise levels in localities
growing faster than the conurbation average. The continued rise in the
use of power by industry will also raise the noise potential from this
source unless control is exercised. Encouragingly, the importance of
land use planning and especially development control in reducing both
industrial and neighbourhood noise problems is now much more
generally recognised.[148, 149]

Of potentially far greater concern are the noise implications of the
projected increase in car ownership and road traffic in the conurbation.
As mentioned in Chapter 2, the 1966 Transportation Study predicted an
increase in pcu trips by 1984 ranging between 30% and 180% for individual districts and of 80% for the conurbation as a whole. Since the
precise pattern of these trips cannot be accurately predicted it is not
possible to determine how the increase in traffic volumes will be geographically distributed. Given, however, the magnitude of the projected
increase it is difficult to envisage that noise levels will fail to increase in
all parts of the sub-region unless controls are applied to the noise
emissions from the individual vehicle. It has been estimated that,
without such controls, the proportion of the population in the country
experiencing undesirable road traffic noise levels will increase from the
19–46% mentioned earlier, in 1970, to 30–61% in 1980.[141] As in the case
of neighbourhood and industrial noise, land use planning, especially the
control of housing, schools and hospital development can be used
partially to mitigate the effects of these noise increases on the receptor
population. This type of control, coupled with new compensation
schemes, now receives considerable official encouragement.[147, 149, 150]

The projected rapid increase in future air travel[151] and its likely impact on the noise climate around Ringway airport, is also the source of considerable concern. Although aircraft movements are not increasing at the same rate as the number of passengers, and the latest generation of sub-sonic planes are less noisy than their immediate predecessors, some further increase in the daytime noise climate is expected during the first half of the 1970s.[144] Thereafter the likely situation is less clear given the uncertainty about the construction of a second runway and changes in the number and noise characteristics of individual plane movements. The most optimistic assumption is that there will be a stabilisation of noise levels during the second half of the decade.[152] The previously described control on development in the vicinity of the airport will therefore be needed to contain the noise annoyance which the airport will continue to cause in the adjacent local authority areas.

7 A general appraisal

This final chapter is divided into three sections. The first draws together the local authority data available on air, land, water and noise pollution and, using a composite pollution index, analyses the main differences in the overall pollution situation between local authority areas within Greater Manchester. The second section compares pollution in Greater Manchester as a whole with that in other regions in the country and summarises likely future trends. The final section sets out the study's main conclusions of policy significance to the reorganised pollution control authorities and describes some of the ways in which area studies of this kind might be further developed to become more useful tools for environmental management purposes. It concludes by discussing procedures for improving environmental quality in highly polluted areas.

Pollution differences between local authorities
Both quantitative and qualitative evidence of differences in the levels of air, land, water and noise pollution between the local authorities within Greater Manchester have been presented in the preceding four chapters. The six pollutant measures for which recent quantitative data are available for a substantial number of local authorities are as follows: ground-level smoke and sulphur dioxide concentrations for winter 1970/1 (38 observations each), the proportion of local authority areas occupied by active and derelict spoil heaps and tips in 1972 (61 observations), road vehicle pollutant emissions and noise levels using 1966 traffic densities as a proxy variable (43 observations) and 1970 river and canal quality (70 and 44 observations respectively). These six statistical series have been used to construct a single composite pollution index for each local authority within Greater Manchester.

The composite pollution index
The construction of a composite pollution index raises three related problems: the standardisation of each series of pollutant statistics, the weights to be applied to each series and the incomplete coverage of each

series. The standardisation procedure used influences the weight given to any particular pollution observation in the derivation of the composite index and, in principle, the weight attached to any such observation should reflect the relative importance of the environmental damage which it causes. However, as the preceding chapters have made clear, knowledge of these effects is incomplete and often speculative. In these circumstances, simple standardisation and weighting methods are to be preferred since nothing is gained by using more sophisticated systems. The sensitivity of the results to alternative standardisation and weighting assumptions can, if necessary, be assessed by the reader using the data supplied later in the chapter.

The observed ranges in each statistical series were as follows: smoke 42–262 $\mu g/m^3$, sulphur dioxide 88–249 $\mu g/m^3$, traffic density 0·8–9·9 pcu miles/acre, land pollution 0–18·2% total authority acreage, average river quality 1·0–4·0 and average canal quality 1·0–3·1. These data were standardised by giving the highest observation in each series a value of 100 and the lowest a value of 0 and then adjusting all the intermediate observations in each series to fall on a linear scale (Table 18, in which dashes indicate no river, no canal or no data). It was then assumed that standardised measures of different pollutants should be weighted equally, so that the composite pollution index was obtained by taking the arithmetic mean of those measures available for each local authority. Although the possible range of values of the index is 0–100, the majority fall between 20 and 50 (Table 18).

In fact, there are only 19 authorities for which all six measures of pollution are available (mainly the central and north western county or municipal boroughs). In addition there are 11 authorities having five measures, 14 with four measures, 16 with three measures, 10 with two measures and 1 having only a single measure. (The local authorities for which only one or two measures exist are, without exception, on the periphery of the conurbation.) The method used in constructing the composite pollution index implies that, for each authority, the values of the absent measures are very similar to the mean value of the pollution measures which are available for that authority. In a number of cases this is an acceptable, although approximate, assumption (page 117) which becomes increasingly questionable as the number of pollution measures available for an authority is reduced. This implication should be taken into consideration in interpreting the composite pollution indices for certain of the peripheral authorities.

Local Authority No.	Smoke Concentration	Sulphur Dioxide Concentration	Traffic Density	Land Pollution	River Quality	Canal Quality	Composite Pollution Index
1	58	43	20	5	53	0	30
2	50	56	25	2	40	0	29
3	48	86	77	8	67	10	49
4	48	58	33	5	27	0	28
5	64	87	16	3	80	0	42
6	86	66	100	0	73	0	54
7	20	35	47	8	57	-	33
8	100	66	-	13	77	95	70
9	8	25	18	-	0	48	20
10	35	34	28	9	87	0	32
11	36	62	16	4	100	0	36
12	37	68	47	9	87	48	49
13	-	-	61	10	100	-	57
14	41	100	-	6	37	-	46
15	40	58	15	0	100	0	36
16	35	25	-	51	40	48	40
17	60	99	35	3	97	0	49
18	-	-	-	8	90	0	33
19	59	87	26	4	67	-	49
20	50	73	20	26	83	0	42
21	-	-	44	-	43	48	45
22	39	43	16	0	100	0	33
23	29	53	84	15	70	100	58
24	-	-	66	59	67	0	48
25	-	-	-	40	33	48	40
26	-	-	-	0	33	48	27
27	58	0	22	43	-	-	31
28	-	-	50	14	100	0	41
29	42	25	-	8	0	48	25
30	-	-	28	-	33	-	30
31	-	-	20	3	63	0	22
32	-	-	28	7	100	0	34
33	14	21	37	-	17	-	22
34	-	-	0	12	0	-	4
35	17	35	37	13	100	-	40
36	47	76	49	36	67	0	46

Table 18 Standardised values of air, water, land and noise pollution measures and composite pollution index by local authority

Variations in index between authorities
The value of the composite pollution index for each local authority in Greater Manchester is mapped in Figure 31. Given the limitations in the basic data and the simplifying assumptions involved in the construction

Local Authority Number	Smoke Concentration	Sulphur Dioxide Concentration	Traffic Density	Land Pollution	River Quality	Canal Quality	Composite Pollution Index
37	54	71	36	16	77	0	42
38	17	43	21	-	23	-	26
39	-	-	22	0	33	-	18
40	-	-	-	17	37	-	27
41	63	48	4	14	0	-	26
42	-	-	-	64	33	81	59
43	20	24	-	6	60	-	28
44	38	45	32	3	93	0	35
45	-	-	31	100	0	-	43
46	-	-	-	2	10	0	4
47	-	-	35	20	50	0	26
48	-	-	-	0	87	-	44
49	-	-	-	-	50	0	25
50	-	-	0	3	60	0	16
51	-	-	-	-	67	48	58
52	0	1	28	17	0	-	9
53	20	9	-	1	17	-	12
54	-	-	-	19	100	48	56
55	35	14	-	17	0	-	16
56	-	-	-	50	67	48	55
57	22	44	38	9	70	81	44
58	-	-	-	5	57	0	21
59	46	47	20	17	50	-	36
60	34	65	30	7	33	-	34
61	-	-	-	-	0	-	0
62	-	-	6	-	23	-	15
63	30	56	38	18	17	48	34
64	-	-	-	7	0	86	31
65	-	-	-	3	50	-	26
66	-	-	-	2	100	-	51
67	22	13	-	7	57	-	25
68	-	-	-	2	40	48	30
69	-	-	-	1	33	-	17
70	-	-	-	0	47	48	32
71	-	-	-	-	0	0	0

Table 18 (cont.)

of the index, too much should not be read into the detailed results. However, the broad pattern of the findings is fairly clear.

There are two main areas of high overall pollution in Greater Manchester. The largest is at the centre of the conurbation, consisting of authorities to the west, north, east and south of Salford CB (6). The second is a smaller group of western authorities based upon Wigan CB (8). These two areas are joined by a belt of rather less polluted

authorities which continues to the eastern boundary of the sub-region.
At the other extreme are a number of peripheral authorities, mainly to
the north west, north east and along the southern perimeter of the sub-
region, which have low index values (Figure 31).

Comparison of high and low pollution areas reveals three features

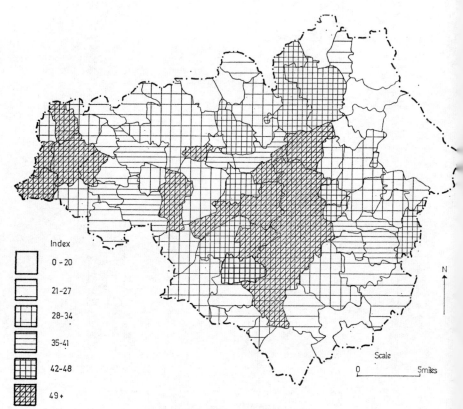

Figure 31   Local authority composite pollution indices

which are of considerable significance to the pollution control objectives
and policies discussed in the final part of this chapter. The ten authorities
with the highest composite pollution indices (the 'top ten') are Wigan
CB (8), Ince-in-Makerfield UD (42), Stretford MB (23), Orrell UD (51),
Farnworth MB (13), Standish-with-Langtree UD (54), Tyldesley UD
(56), Salford CB (6), Billinge and Winstanley UD (66) and Manchester

CB (3). Since only two pollution measures are available for Orrell UD (51) and Billinge and Winstanley UD (66), their inclusion should be regarded with caution.

The 'bottom ten' authorities are Macclesfield RD (71), Crompton UD (34), Littleborough UD (46), Royton UD (52), Saddleworth UD (53), Wilmslow UD (62), Milnrow UD (50), Tottington UD (55), Turton UD (69) and Hazel Grove and Bramhall UD (39). Whitworth UD (61) has been excluded from this group because a single pollution measure was felt to be insufficient to justify its inclusion, especially as it is known to have significant land pollution.[105] These authorities, with two exceptions, are all peripheral to the conurbation and, in a number of cases, their indices were calculated from only two or three pollution measures.

The first notable feature of the 'top ten' local authorities, excepting Billinge and Winstanley UD (66), is that each records two or more high pollution measures and, with the further exception of Orrell UD (51), high pollution levels in two or more environmental media. More generally, there is evidence of a correlation between the spatial distribution of different forms of pollution within the sub-region. Smoke concentrations were found to be closely correlated with sulphur dioxide concentrations ($\alpha = 0.0005$) and with average river quality (significant at the 97.5% level) but not to be significantly correlated with the other pollution measures. Sulphur dioxide concentrations are also correlated with river pollution ($\alpha = 0.005$) but are not correlated with other pollutants except smoke. Traffic densities are not related to smoke and sulphur dioxide levels but are positively correlated with river quality ($\alpha = 0.05$) and, negatively, with canal quality ($\alpha = 0.025$). River quality, apart from its correlation with the various air and noise pollution measures is negatively correlated with canal quality (Chapter 5). Only the land pollution measure is not significantly correlated with any of the other pollutants. These relationships underline the multi-media nature of the pollution problem which is an important consideration when devising suitable environmental management schemes for polluted areas.

The second feature of the 'top ten' authorities, again excepting Billinge and Winstanley UD (66), is that they have population and industrial employment (SIC Orders 2–18) densities substantially higher than the conurbation averages. Conversely, the 'bottom ten' authorities, excepting Crompton UD (34) and Royton UD (52), have lower than average densities. Table 19 shows that the mean densities (in persons per acre) of the most polluted authorities are about four times those of the least polluted areas.

	Population Density	Industrial Employment Density	Socio-economic grouping Index	Car Owner-ship
Top 10	12.2	3.8	373	113
Bottom 10	3.1	1.1	330	208

Table 19 Average values of various characteristics of the 'top 10' and 'bottom 10' local authorities, 1966

These differences partially explain the relative position of the two groups of authorities in the composite pollution index league table, since there is a marked correlation between the index and such waste generation variables as population density, total employment density and industrial employment density (see Appendix). In addition, differences in these variables are likely to be responsible for variations in some of the supplementary measures of pollution (e.g. industrial and domestic noise and air pollution, and domestic, industrial and, perhaps, agricultural solid waste disposal problems). Only aircraft noise (Chapter 6) does not obviously follow this pattern. The low pollution authorities also tend to be located favourably with respect to waste diffusion. They are generally situated on the relatively clean upper reaches of rivers at the edge of the conurbation and thus benefit from a net export of both water-borne and air-borne wastes. The association between the location, population and industrial characteristics of areas and their overall pollution level is an additional factor in formulating environmental control schemes (including town planning measures) for high pollution authorities.

Again, there appear to be important differences between the socio-economic structure and income levels of the two groups of authorities. The high population areas tend to have below average car ownership levels (cars/1000 population) and an above average proportion of manual workers in their resident population (high socio-economic grouping index; Table 19). The low pollution authorities in the south of the conurbation display precisely the opposite socio-economic and car ownership characteristics, although not all such authorities in the north do so.

Nevertheless, in general, there is a significant correlation between the socio-economic grouping indices and the car ownerships of the various Greater Manchester authorities and their composite pollution indices (see Appendix). This feature raises questions of equity which are central to public policy, not only because the 'disadvantaged areas' are experiencing the highest levels of pollution but because part of this pollution is originating from other, often higher income, areas (page 127).

Pollution in the Greater Manchester sub-region

Before examining the policy and organisational implications of the spatial distribution of pollution within Greater Manchester, it is desirable to place the sub-regional situation in its regional and national context and to take account of recent trends and forecasts of conurbation pollution levels.

Regional and national comparisons

The North West is the most heavily industrialised and densely populated region in the country.[5] In 1970/1 the average smoke concentration in the urban areas of the North West was second only to those in the North region, and the equivalent sulphur dioxide concentrations were higher than in any other region (although exceeded in the Greater London sub-region).[41] The North West also has the highest traffic density (1966 vehicle mileage/acre) of all the regions, although again exceeded by Greater London.[153] 1970 derelict land statistics suggest that the percentage of land occupied by derelict spoil heaps and tips in the North West (and indeed by derelict land generally) is greater than in other regions.[130] Finally, of all the regions, the North West has the largest proportion of its rivers in a badly polluted condition (classes 3 and 4) although its canal quality is better than the national average.[134] (See Table 20, in which all the 'country' statistics relate to the UK except traffic density (Great Britain), river and canal quality (England and Wales) and land pollution (England).)

Yet, in the case of smoke and sulphur dioxide (1970/1 annual average concentration in $\mu g/m^3$), traffic density, land pollution (1970 derelict spoil heap percentage) and river pollution (1970 average river quality), the situation is considerably worse in Greater Manchester than in the North West as a whole (Table 20). In addition, industrial employment and residential densities (1966 persons/acre) are high in comparison

	Smoke	Sulphur Dioxide	Traffic Density	Derelict Heaps & Tips	River Quality	Canal Quality	Industrial Density	Population Density
Greater Manchester	101	142	9.1	0.76	2.7	1.5	2.2	8.0
North West	81	125	6.2	0.25	1.9	1.5	0.8	3.4
Country as a Whole	60	102	1.9	0.11	1.4	1.8	0.2	0.9

Table 20 Values of various pollution measures in Greater Manchester, the North West region and the country as a whole

with the North West and the UK[15] indicating that air pollution and noise from these sources are likely to be at least as great as elsewhere in the country (Table 20). However, the condition of canals (1970 average canal quality) in Greater Manchester is similar to the regional average and, while the proportion of people affected by aircraft noise is higher in the conurbation than in the region and in the country as a whole, as with traffic noise, London is worse affected.

Unfortunately, the obtainable data do not indicate how pollution in Greater Manchester compares with that in other provincial conurbations such as the West Midlands or Tyne and Wear. The available evidence nevertheless points to the sub-region being amongst the most heavily polluted in the country and the situation in the 'top ten' polluted authority areas within the conurbation should be viewed in this context.

In addition to being much more polluted than the North West region as a whole, Greater Manchester exports wastes to it in every medium. A proportion of the air-borne wastes generated within the sub-region are diffused over the surrounding rural areas, particularly those to the north east (in the direction of the prevailing winds: page 47). About 40,000 dry tons of sewage sludge from the conurbation are deposited, with various industrial wastes, in Liverpool Bay (Chapter 4). The river water flowing into the area is generally clean, whereas the large quantities of water flowing out of Greater Manchester are grossly polluted (Chapter 5). The number of people living outside the conurbation affected by noise from road traffic generated within it is probably greater than that of sub-region residents subject to noise from traffic generated externally. Finally, numerous residents outside Greater Manchester (for example, those living in Knutsford and Mobberley) suffer from noise created by the airport within it (Figure 29).

Trends in pollution in Greater Manchester

It is important to recognise that, as elsewhere in the country, there have been considerable improvements in the levels of a number of pollutants in Greater Manchester during the last decade. Annual average smoke and sulphur dioxide concentrations fell by 50% and 40% respectively during the 1960s. Over the same period, grit and dust concentrations at the more limited number of measuring sites in the conurbation appear to have fallen by a factor of two. These changes have been associated with better visibility and more sunshine and (although less conclusively established) with improvements in human health, increased variety of bird life, reduced plant damage and diminished soiling of materials within the sub-region (Chapter 3). Similarly, there has been a significant if not striking improvement in river quality between 1958 and 1970, with a consequent increase in the proportion of river mileage capable of supporting fish life (Chapter 5).

Elsewhere the trend is less encouraging. According to the official statistics,[127] the acreage of derelict spoil heaps and tips in Greater Manchester has increased since 1966, although this may not necessarily be a true reflection of the situation (Chapter 4). On the other hand, there is no doubt that noise levels have risen rapidly during the last decade due mainly to the growth of air and road traffic (Chapter 6). The increase in road traffic has also been responsible for a very considerable rise in vehicle emissions during the last decade.

The trend in pollution levels within Greater Manchester as a whole has therefore been mixed. Unfortunately, it is not possible to describe with any confidence the equivalent trends within the different local authorities in the conurbation. In certain cases (e.g. sulphur dioxide concentrations in Salford CB (6), Figure 14) pollution levels have fallen faster than the conurbation average, but in others (e.g. river pollution) the centrally located high pollution areas have experienced little improvement (Chapter 5). Similarly, road traffic pollutants have generally increased more rapidly in the inner authorities (with the exception of the central business district) than in the peripheral areas (Chapter 2). It is therefore possible that, overall, the difference between the most and least polluted areas in Greater Manchester may even have increased during the last decade. This disparity adds further significance to the equity issue discussed in the final section of the chapter.

Forecasts

Although there will probably only be a modest (2%) increase in the resident population of the sub-region and a small decline in total employment (2%) over the next decade (Chapter 2) total production and consumer spending will almost certainly continue to increase by at least 2% each year.[15] In the absence of controls these increases will lead to a considerably greater generation of wastes which, given the high population density and intensive use of land in many parts of the conurbation may raise acute disposal problems. Despite these increases, controls already in existence or likely to be implemented shortly should ensure the reduction of certain types of pollution.

In the area as a whole, it is expected that both mean smoke and, to a lesser extent, sulphur dioxide concentrations will continue to decline, probably to less than 60 $\mu g/m^3$ and 100 $\mu g/m^3$ respectively by the early 1980s (Chapter 3). Stricter limits on industrial process emissions are expected to reduce waste/output ratios although the controls may not always be sufficient to lower local pollutant concentrations where considerable industrial expansion (or a new complex) arises. River quality is forecast to continue to improve although at the end of the decade the percentage of the sub-region's river mileage capable of supporting fish life will still be less than the 1970 national average (Table 15). Programmed derelict land reclamation schemes are expected to considerably reduce the magnitude of this problem during the next decade (Chapter 4).

The most serious future pollution problems within Greater Manchester are likely to be associated with road, and possibly air, transport and with the disposal of solid and semi-solid wastes. The number of pcu trips is expected to increase by about 80% in the SELNEC area between 1966 and 1984 (Chapter 2), and in the absence of strict controls on emissions of both noise and atmospheric pollutants, it will prove extremely difficult to prevent further deterioration in environmental quality from this source. The noise climate around Ringway Airport is unlikely to improve until the latter part of the decade when quieter engines may be in more widespread use (Chapter 6).

Quantities of most types of solid waste generated are expected to increase over the next decade. In addition, because of stricter controls over river pollution, the amounts of sludge resulting from the treatment of sewage and industrial effluents will probably also rise. The environmentally acceptable disposal of these wastes, given the shortage of tipping facilities and stricter land use planning controls on tipping practice and reclamation, will require comprehensive solid waste management schemes that do not exist at the moment.

The manner in which these future trends might affect the different parts of Greater Manchester is necessarily largely speculative. Continued reductions in smoke and sulphur dioxide concentrations and improvements in river quality must eventually benefit the disadvantaged, high pollution, areas in addition to the other areas within the conurbation and major increases in traffic densities and solid waste disposals may occur in the outer areas, once the existing capacities of the inner areas have been fully utilised. Whether these changes will reduce disparities in environmental quality within the conurbation and, if so, how soon this will occur, is unclear. However, it appears certain that Greater Manchester's pollution will remain serious, although changing in nature, for the foreseeable future unless further and more effective control measures are taken and that, at least initially, pollution problems will be most evident in the lower income areas in the centre and west of the conurbation.

Pollution control policy and implementation
This final section reviews three related aspects of pollution control in Greater Manchester which are also of wider application: the organisational structure for controlling pollution within the sub-region, the future use of pollution models in policy formulation and the implementation of priority control programmes for disadvantaged areas.

Organisational structure
Pollution control can be effected at a number of stages in the pollution progress (Figure 1) but within Greater Manchester these controls are currently exercised on different pollutants by a considerable number of separate authorities. The integrated nature of the pollution process, as described in Chapter 1, is thus reflected in a coincidence neither in control over particular pollutants nor in jurisdiction over geographical areas (Figure 10). This problem has been further compounded by the absence of a clear consensus among the controlling authorities on pollution control objectives,[154] methods or implementation.[35]

The administration of pollution control will undergo substantial change in 1974 when a new two-tier system of local government is introduced and the control of the water cycle (with the exception of canals) comes under the jurisdiction of new regional water authorities.

One of the effects of these changes will be to reduce considerably the number of separate organisations involved in pollution control within the sub-region, a rationalisation which is apparent on comparing Figures 10 and 32.

Despite the smaller number of authorities concerned, the re-organised

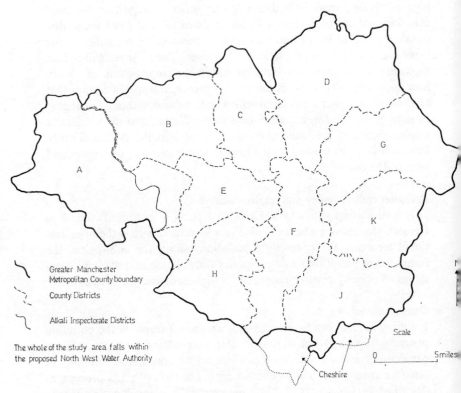

Greater Manchester
Metropolitan County boundary

County Districts

Alkali Inspectorate Districts

The whole of the study area falls within
the proposed North West Water Authority

Cheshire

Scale

0   5miles

Figure 32   Pollution control authorities in Greater Manchester, 1974

structure does not ensure a unified system of pollution control. The metropolitan district council will have responsibilities for refuse collection, for certain aspects of clean air and noise abatement and for other public health functions, including sewerage, currently administered by 69 Greater Manchester local authorities. They will also have many planning functions including the implementation of most development control. The metropolitan county council will be responsible for structure plan preparation and certain other planning functions, for refuse disposal, for highway investment and for public transport provision.[11] The North West Water Authority will administer sewage treatment and disposal, water supply and river pollution control[37] whilst Her Majesty's Clean Air and Alkali Inspectorate will retain control over emissions from registered works.

Furthermore, within the new local authorities, jurisdiction over pollution control may be shared between a number of different departments. Therefore, if a unified system of control over all types of pollution is to be established, priority should be given to the formulation of agreed schemes of co-ordination of pollution control between the authorities and departments concerned. Such agreements will need to include the objectives of pollution control and the setting of environmental quality standards for particular localities as well as procedural arrangements for consultation, etc. A case has been made for the structure planning authority to co-ordinate such arrangements,[155] but the reaching of an early agreement is at present more important than the precise allocation of co-ordination responsibilities.

Sub-regional pollution models
The attainment of a unified system of pollution control will not occur quickly, given the short-term disruption of re-organisation and the traditional reliance of the controlling authorities on fairly pragmatic methods for dealing with specific pollution problems in particular environmental media. The development of a working model of the pollution process within the sub-region (incorporating air, land, water and noise pollution) could be very helpful in facilitating the change to more comprehensive waste control management schemes. It could be used, for example, to predict the likely future impact on environmental quality of major policy decisions (e.g. planning applications for housing re-development schemes, airport expansions, hypermarkets, industrial estates, etc.). Similarly, once environmental standards have been set for particular areas, such a model could be employed to identify and evaluate the alternative control authority policy measures to implement them. In short, the sub-regional pollution study might perform a similar role to that of the transportation study in urban transport planning by providing a comprehensive basis for pollution forecasting, land use and environmental quality decision-making.

However, at present, pollution models are not so well developed as the corresponding urban transportation models. This study has outlined the structure of one such model (Appendix) and the extent to which it can already be employed to identify pollution problems within a conurbation. The usefulness of the model would be greatly enhanced by two types of development.

Firstly, improvements are needed in the data base. As a preliminary step it would be desirable to undertake a comprehensive review of pollution monitoring systems within the sub-region. This review might well establish the need for better data on solid wastes and their disposal, for improvements of a selective nature in the recording of smoke and sulphur dioxide concentrations and for more complete measurement of a wide range of environmental parameters in highly polluted areas. For example, information about concentrations of oxides of nitrogen, lead, etc. in the atmosphere, noise levels from a wide range of sources and amounts of heavy metals, pesticides, etc. in rivers, canals and enclosed waters would be invaluable and might be collected on a selected representative area basis. Information which is at present restricted to the relevant control authority (e.g. about effluents to rivers and certain emissions to air) should be made generally available. Pollution and other relevant data (e.g. land use records) could be stored centrally in a sub-regional data bank maintained by one of the main co-ordinating authorities, where it would be available both for improving the working model and for more specific control purposes.

Secondly, further clarification is needed of those relationships within the pollution process which are of policy significance. These include:

(a) the relationship between the residential and industrial characteristics of an area and the type and quantity of waste it generates. An inventory of the air-borne, water-borne and solid wastes and noise produced by different land uses would be of great benefit to the pollution control authorities and especially to town planners;

(b) the relationship between the disposal and ultimate fate of wastes released to the environment at different points within the sub-region. Apart from data on levels of pollution, supporting information about receptors and the functional relationship between pollution and effect need to be established to estimate the ensuing damage; and

(c) the repercussions of specific control measures on wastes discharged to a particular medium or on the quantities of waste released to other media and in other parts of the sub-region. For example, stricter planning controls on the tipping of solid wastes encourage the use of incineration, generating air-borne wastes which require quantification. The clarification of these relationships might be a co-operative exercise involving university research as well as investigation by the various controlling authorities.

The disadvantaged areas

The development of comprehensive waste management policies based upon modelling the pollution process in the sub-region will take some years. In the meantime, a prima facie case has been established earlier in this chapter for taking action in the disadvantaged areas which are experiencing relatively high levels of pollution in two or more environmental media.

The first requirement is a more detailed examination of pollution levels in the areas identified earlier, supplemented by further monitoring. The results will almost certainly show considerable variations in such areas. The little evidence available from this study (e.g. SELNEC district traffic density and aircraft noise data) suggests that the direct relationship between pollution and income applies within local authorities as well as between them. These variations require closer investigation. It would then be necessary to assess the likely damage (including that to amenity) caused by the prevailing pollution.

If damage is found to be significant, then alternative means of reducing pollution levels will need evaluation. For example, the involuntary import of pollution from other areas (e.g. from through traffic and poor quality inflowing rivers) could be reduced by traffic measurement schemes, by-pass roads and new priorities in river improvement schemes. The costs of implementing such policies should not fall upon the disadvantaged areas.

High pollution levels in these areas are also linked to their high residential and employment densities, which can be gradually reduced by redevelopment, rehabilitation and improvement programmes. Waste generation rates can also be lowered by imposing stricter effluent and emission controls. However, unless other corrective action is taken, these measures could affect employment opportunities in the areas and impose real costs on the communities affected.

The limited evidence available suggests that pollution reduction is not considered so important by low income groups as it is by more affluent communities[156] and that such groups are not prepared to pay as much to avoid pollution as higher income communities.[151] They also tend to complain less about pollution problems—the pollution complaints ratio in the ten most polluted areas in Greater Manchester was well below the average in the conurbation as a whole, whereas that in the least polluted authorities was similar to the average.[53] These findings, however, need to be interpreted cautiously since they may arise from inexperience of clean environments, lower purchasing power and deprived educational backgrounds; all manifestations of the disadvantaged areas. It is therefore possible that improvements in environmental quality should form part of a more general policy devoted to the reduction of inequalities within the sub-region.

These issues are clearly central to the strategic planning of the conurbation, and the formulation of appropriate policies to reduce pollution in the disadvantaged areas should be an important structure plan priority for the new metropolitan county council. More detailed land use plans and development control could then be employed to implement these policies at metropolitan district level.[157]

Finally, after standards have been set for these areas and the most appropriate means for their attainment identified, it is essential that they continue to be implemented. The evidence in Greater Manchester suggests that it is not possible to rely upon complaints from the general public in disadvantaged areas to alert the controlling authorities about pollution problems. Special attention to environmental inspection is therefore required and, given the multi-media nature of the problem revealed in this study, this may be best afforded by a general purpose inspectorate[158] with wide ranging powers of investigation and enforcement.

Appendix

A number of models have been constructed in the past for air-borne wastes,[159] water-borne wastes,[160] solid wastes[161] and noise.[151] To date there have, however, been few attempts to build an integrated waste/pollution model[162] although the construction of spatial models which incorporate environmental sub-systems is becoming more common.[163] Empirical studies of the total pollution process have rarely been undertaken on a spatial basis. The most comprehensive review of different types of pollution within a particular area relates to Tokyo metropolitan county[164] but no effort was made to show the relationship of pollutants to the remainder of the pollution process or to examine them in relation to the characteristics of the metropolitan area. A less well documented account of pollution problems in London has been prepared,[165] again without any relationship to the spatial base being established.

Structure of the pollution process

The pollution process in a sub-regional area may be represented by a set of algebraic equations. Consider that the area consists of n zones, each separately denoted $i = 1 \cdots n$. Waste (W) consists of gaseous and particulate air-borne waste (W^a), solid waste (W^b), water-borne waste (W^c) and noise (W^d). (Wastes such as pesticides, radiation, heavy metals, etc., fall into one or other of these categories.) Thus in zone i:

$$W_i = W_i^a + W_i^b + \mathbf{W}_i^c + W_i^d \tag{1}$$

Each type of waste has a number of constituents. For example, air-borne waste might be divided into smoke, sulphur dioxide and large particulate matter, etc. In general:

$$W^a = W^{a_1} + W^{a_2} + W^{a_3} + \cdots$$
$$W^b = W^{b_1} + W^{b_2} + W^{b_3} + \cdots$$
$$\cdots\cdots\cdots\cdots\cdots\cdots\cdots$$

or, for zone i:

$$W_i^a = W_i^{a_1} + W_i^{a_2} + W_i^{a_3} + \cdots$$
$$W_i^b = W_i^{b_1} + W_i^{b_2} + W_i^{b_3} + \cdots \tag{2}$$
$$\cdots\cdots\cdots\cdots\cdots\cdots\cdots$$

The basic determinants of waste generation in an area are the size of its population (N), its socio-economic characteristics (car ownership, income, socio-economic status, etc.) collectively represented by S, the degree of industrial activity in the area (I) and the composition of the activity (C). Waste can thus be shown to be a function of these determinants:

$$W^a = f^a(N, S, I, C)$$
$$W^b = f^b(N, S, I, C)$$
$$\dots\dots\dots\dots\dots$$

The function can be expressed, in the case of air-borne wastes in zone i, by the following equation:

$$W_i^a = e + gN_i + hS_i + kI_i + lC_i \tag{3}$$

where e is a constant and g, h, k and l are technical waste coefficients. Similar equations with different constants and technical coefficients can be employed to represent the generation of wastes released to the other media.

If P denotes the pollution concentrations, then P_i^a represents the air pollution ground level concentration in zone i, and $P_i^{a_1}$ the smoke concentration, $P_i^{a_2}$ the sulphur dioxide concentration, and so on. Pollution of a particular medium is a function of the waste generated in a zone, the import of substances in the same medium from other zones or from outside the study area (X) and of any transfers of substances from other media (Y) together with the diffusion characteristics of the zone (B). Thus, for air pollution:

$$P^a = f(W^a, X^a, Y^a, B^a)$$

In zone i, air pollution can be represented by an equation of the following form:

$$P_i^a = m + B_i^a(W_i^a + X_i^a + Y_i^a) \tag{4}$$

where m is a constant and B_i^a is the diffusion coefficient. B is necessarily an extremely complex parameter, and will not only vary from medium to medium and in the detailed representation of the diffusion of W, X and Y, but may vary from pollutant to pollutant within a medium and from zone to zone.

If damage is represented by D, then D_i^a denotes the damage associated with air pollution in zone i and this may be disaggregated to $D_i^{a_1}$, $D_i^{a_2}$, $D_i^{a_3}$, etc., in order to distinguish the damage from different pollutants.

Damage is a function of pollution dose (which is determined by concentration and duration of exposure) and the characteristics of receptors. If it is assumed that current damage is a function of current pollution concentration, and that receptor characteristics can be denoted by a single variable, R, then:

$$D^a = f(P^a, R^a)$$

and in zone i:

$$D_i^a = n + pP_i^a R_i^a \qquad (5)$$

where n is a constant having a value less than or equal to zero, since damage will only occur when a threshold has been exceeded by the appropriate values of P_i^a and R_i^a. The constant and technical coefficient will vary from pollutant to pollutant as well as from medium to medium.

Equations 1–5 describe, in algebraic form, the main structural components of the highly simplified pollution process within a sub-region and the ways in which they are linked with each other. All these components can be represented in a much more realistic (and, therefore, complex) manner. For example, the relationships between the pollution level and damage may need to take duration as well as intensity of exposure and damage into account. Similarly, the technical coefficients may also need to be varied from one group of zones to the next, or even between zones.

In addition to estimating present pollution levels and damage, the modelling of the pollution process might be extended to forecast these components at some future date. This would involve forecasting the values of the basic determinants N, S, I and C and any changes in the constants and technical coefficients to obtain estimates of future waste levels. These, together with forecast changes in such explanatory variables as X, Y and R and in the associated constants and coefficients could then be used to calculate approximate pollution and damage levels.

However, the limitations in data described in Chapter 1 prevent even the simplified representation of the pollution process being converted, at present, into a full working model. Nevertheless, it has been possible to explore some of these relationships in the chapters of this book and in certain cases, to determine a number of technical coefficients (below). With the continued improvement in data availability it should be possible in the future to refine these results and extend them to the point where models of the pollution process in sub-regional areas become operational.

Regression results

The following equations summarise the empirical results obtained from the various regression analyses described earlier in the book. The variables all relate to different local authorities or different years and the regression equations consequently never require the subscripts used in equations 1–5 to distinguish between local authorities. Subscripts are, however, employed to denote differences in the type of variable represented (e.g. cars, district populations and mean household income). Simple regression equations (one dependent and one independent variable) are accompanied by the Pearsonian correlation coefficient (r) and its significance (α) when tested using the Student statistic (t). All these equations are significant at the 95% level ($\alpha = 0.05$). Multiple regression equations (more than one independent variable) are shown with the corrected 't' values for each variable coefficient, together with the $\bar{R}^2$ value (the percentage of the variance explained after adjustment for degrees of freedom). Each set of equations is prefaced by a cross-reference to the page on which they are discussed.

Motor vehicle emissions and SELNEC district socio-economic characteristics, 1966 (page 38)

$$W^{a_4} = 7500 - 28S_1 \qquad r = -0.44 \qquad \alpha = 0.0005$$
$$W^{a_4} = 7900 - 4.2S_2 \qquad r = -0.22 \qquad \alpha = 0.05$$
$$W^{a_4} = 1600 + 0.23S_3 \qquad r = 0.38 \qquad \alpha = 0.0025$$

where W^{a_4} = pcu miles/sq. mile
S_1 = number of cars/1000 district population
S_2 = mean household income (£)
S_3 = population/sq. mile

Smoke and sulphur dioxide concentrations and local authority characteristics, 1966 (page 48)

$$P^{a_{10}} = 150 + 3.7S_4 \qquad r = 0.46 \qquad \alpha = 0.0025$$
$$P^{a_{10}} = 160 + 5.3I \qquad r = 0.40 \qquad \alpha = 0.01$$
$$P^{a_{11}} = 15 + 0.079S_5 \qquad r = 0.57 \qquad \alpha = 0.0005$$
$$P^{a_{20}} = 350 - 0.88S_6 \qquad r = -0.61 \qquad \alpha = 0.0005$$
$$P^{a_{20}} = 180 + 14C_1 \qquad r = 0.50 \qquad \alpha = 0.0025$$
$$P^{a_{10}} = 173 + 9.1C_1 - 0.45S_6$$
$$\phantom{P^{a_{10}} = 173} (11.6) (2.6) (1.1) \qquad\qquad \bar{R}^2 = 0.13$$
$$P^{a_{10}} = 158 + 4.2S_4 - 0.57S_7$$
$$\phantom{P^{a_{10}} = 158} (9.3) (3.0) (1.4) \qquad\qquad \bar{R}^2 = 0.18$$

where $P^{a}{}_{10}$ = winter 1965/6 average smoke concentration (μg/m³)

$P^{a}{}_{11}$ = summer 1966 average smoke concentration (μg/m³)

$P^{a}{}_{20}$ = winter 1965/6 average SO$_2$ concentration (μg/m³)

S_4 = population/acre

S_5 = socio-economic grouping index

S_6 = number of cars/1000 authority population

S_7 = percentage of premises smoke controlled

I = total employment/acre

C_1 = employment in SIC Orders 2–18/acre

Visibility, 1961–8, and hours of sunshine, 1949–70, and pollution concentrations in those years (page 52)

$$D_1^a = 2{\cdot}7 + 0{\cdot}047P^{a}{}_{12} \qquad r = \ \ 0{\cdot}89 \qquad \alpha = 0{\cdot}01$$
$$D_2^a = 4{\cdot}8 + 0{\cdot}056P^{a}{}_{13} \qquad r = \ \ 0{\cdot}51 \qquad \alpha = 0{\cdot}05$$
$$D_3^a = 120 - 0{\cdot}12P^{a}{}_{12} \qquad r = -0{\cdot}54 \qquad \alpha = 0{\cdot}0125$$

where D_1^a = number of days with visibility less than 1000 m at 0900 hours GMT at the Weather Centre during November–January

D_2^a = number of days with visibility less than 1000 m at 0900 hours GMT at the airport during the winter

D_3^a = number of hours of sunshine during November–January

$P^{a}{}_{12}$ = average smoke concentrations in the city centre during November–January

$P^{a}{}_{13}$ = average smoke concentrations at the airport during the winter 1961–8

Mortality, 1970, and local authority socio-economic characteristics, 1966, and pollution in 1970 and preceding years (page 55)

$$D_4^a = 11 + 0{\cdot}028P^{a}{}_{14} \qquad r = 0{\cdot}46 \qquad \alpha = 0{\cdot}005$$
$$D_4^a = 8{\cdot}3 + 0{\cdot}22P^{a}{}_{16} \qquad r = 0{\cdot}60 \qquad \alpha = 0{\cdot}0005$$
$$D_4^a = 8{\cdot}6 + 0{\cdot}039P^{a}{}_{21} \qquad r = 0{\cdot}57 \qquad \alpha = 0{\cdot}0005$$
$$D_4^a = 13 + 0{\cdot}086S_4 \qquad r = 0{\cdot}24 \qquad \alpha = 0{\cdot}025$$
$$D_4^a = -2{\cdot}6 + 0{\cdot}047S_5 \qquad r = 0{\cdot}65 \qquad \alpha = 0{\cdot}0005$$
$$D_4^a = 18 - 0{\cdot}024S_6 \qquad r = -0{\cdot}67 \qquad \alpha = 0{\cdot}0005$$
$$D_5^a = 0{\cdot}026 + 0{\cdot}0038P^{a}{}_{15} \qquad r = 0{\cdot}46 \qquad \alpha = 0{\cdot}005$$
$$D_5^a = 0{\cdot}012 + 0{\cdot}0042P^{a}{}_{22} \qquad r = 0{\cdot}64 \qquad \alpha = 0{\cdot}0005$$
$$D_5^a = -2{\cdot}1 + 0{\cdot}0081S_5 \qquad r = 0{\cdot}60 \qquad \alpha = 0{\cdot}0005$$
$$D_6^a = 0{\cdot}004 + 0{\cdot}005P^{a}{}_{16} \qquad r = 0{\cdot}84 \qquad \alpha = 0{\cdot}0001$$

$$D_6^a = 0.0095 + 0.0041P^{a_{22}} \qquad r = 0.62 \qquad \alpha = 0.0005$$
$$D_7^a = 0.19 + 0.002P^{a_{22}} \qquad r = 0.62 \qquad \alpha = 0.0005$$
$$D_7^a = 0.24 + 0.001P^{a_{23}} \qquad r = 0.40 \qquad \alpha = 0.05$$
$$D_7^a = 0.39 + 0.0026S_5 \qquad r = 0.51 \qquad \alpha = 0.0005$$

$$D_4^a = 2.6 - 0.057S_4 + 0.019S_5 + 0.023P^{a_{16}} - 0.0023P^{a_{23}}$$
$$\quad\ (0.7)\ (1.2) \qquad (1.5) \qquad (3.0) \qquad\ (0.4) \qquad \bar{R}^2 = 0.43$$
$$D_5^a = -1.0 + 0.014S_4 + 0.0038S_5 + 0.0015P^{a_{22}}$$
$$\qquad\quad (2.0) \qquad (3.5) \qquad (1.5) \qquad\qquad \bar{R}^2 = 0.55$$

where D_4^a = TAM—total mortality (see page 56)

D_5^a = AMR (bronchitis and emphysema)

D_6^a = CMR (bronchitis and emphysema)

D_7^a = CMR (lung cancer)

$P^{a_{14}}$ = 1969/70 annual average smoke concentration

$P^{a_{15}}$ = 1969/70 winter average smoke concentration

$P^{a_{16}}$ = 1963/4 winter average smoke concentration

$P^{a_{21}}$ = 1969/70 annual average SO_2 concentration

$P^{a_{22}}$ = 1969/70 winter average SO_2 concentration

$P^{a_{23}}$ = 1963/4 winter average SO_2 concentration

S_4 = population/acre

S_5 = socio-economic grouping index

S_6 = number of cars/1000 authority population

Agricultural waste, 1970, and local authority population density, 1966 (page 72)

$$W_1^b = 4.7 - 0.14S_4 \qquad r = -0.33 \qquad \alpha = 0.005$$
$$W_2^b = 0.0025 + 0.0011S_4 \qquad r = \quad 0.60 \qquad \alpha = 0.005$$

where W_1^b = wet weight of waste (tons/acre)

W_2^b = dry weight of phosphorus (tons agricultural acre)

S_3 = population/acre

Percentage of land occupied by active and derelict spoil heaps and tips, 1972, and local authority socio-economic grouping index, 1966 (page 80)

$$P_1^b = -16 + 0.0052S_5 \qquad r = 0.32 \qquad \alpha = 0.025$$

where P_1^b = percentage of land occupied by active and derelict spoil heaps and tips

S_5 = socio-economic grouping index

Aqueous waste, 1970, and local authority sewage works catchment population (1970) and industrial characteristics, 1966 (page 84)

$$W^{c_1} = 0{\cdot}66 - 0{\cdot}03N + 1{\cdot}01C_2 + 1{\cdot}88C_3 + 0{\cdot}41C_4 + 1{\cdot}12C_5$$
$$(1{\cdot}8) \quad (3{\cdot}6) \quad (2{\cdot}3) \quad (5{\cdot}0) \quad (3{\cdot}1) \quad (2{\cdot}2) \quad \bar{R}^2 = 0{\cdot}55$$

where W^{c_1} = Biochemical oxygen demand (BOD) load (lbs/day)

N = population served by sewage works

C_2 = employment in the chemicals industry

C_3 = employment in the metal industry

C_4 = employment in the textile industry

C_5 = employment in the paper industry

River quality, 1970, and quality of inflowing water and local authority aqueous water discharges, 1970 (page 89)

$$P^c = 1{\cdot}3 + 0{\cdot}48X^c + 0{\cdot}0004W^{c_2}$$
$$(4{\cdot}1) \ (4{\cdot}3) \qquad (1{\cdot}7) \qquad\qquad \bar{R}^2 = 0{\cdot}30$$

where P^c = average river quality

X^c = average quality of river flowing into the local authority

W^{c_2} = BOD load/day/mile (lbs)

Composite pollution index and local authority characteristics, 1966 (page 118)

$P = \quad 23 + 1{\cdot}34S_4$	$r = \quad 0{\cdot}51$	$\alpha = 0{\cdot}0005$
$P = \ -28 + 0{\cdot}175S_5$	$r = \quad 0{\cdot}33$	$\alpha = 0{\cdot}005$
$P = \quad 55 - 0{\cdot}14S_6$	$r = -0{\cdot}47$	$\alpha = 0{\cdot}0005$
$P = \quad 28 + 1{\cdot}9I$	$r = \quad 0{\cdot}42$	$\alpha = 0{\cdot}0005$
$P = \quad 29 + 2{\cdot}9C_1$	$r = \quad 0{\cdot}39$	$\alpha = 0{\cdot}005$

where P = composite pollution index

S_4 = population/acre

S_5 = socio-economic grouping index

S_6 = number of cars/1000 authority population

I = total employment/acre

C_1 = employment in SIC Orders 2–18/acre

References

1 Stern, A.C. (ed.) (1968) *Air Pollution* 3 vols. Academic Press, London.
2 Committee on the Problem of Noise (Wilson Committee) (1963) *Final Report* Cmnd. 2056, HMSO, London.
3 Klein, L. (1967) *River Pollution* 3 vols. Butterworths, London.
4 Royal Commission on Environmental Pollution (1971) *1st Report* Cmnd. 4585, HMSO, London.
5 Central Statistical Office (1972) *Abstract of Regional Statistics 1972* HMSO, London.
6 Royal Ministry for Foreign Affairs and Royal Ministry of Agriculture (1972) *Air pollution across national boundaries* Swedish RMFA & RMA, Stockholm.
7 Pullen, W.A. (ed.) (1971) *The Municipal Year Book 1971* Municipal Journal Ltd., London.
8 Lee, N. and Saunders, P.J.W. (1972) Pollution as a function of affluence and population increase. *In* Cox, P.R. and Peel, J. (eds.) *Population and Pollution* Academic Press, London.
9 Joint Working on Structure Plans for Greater Manchester (1973) *Environment and pollution* Discussion paper, Manchester Corporation, Manchester.
10 Department of the Environment (1971) *Circular 84/71* HMSO, London.
11 *Local Government Act 1972.*
12 Mersey and Weaver River Authority (1967–73) *Annual Report* MWRA, Great Sankey, Warrington.
13 National Air Pollution Control Administration (1969) *The climate of cities* Publication AP-59, Government Printing Office, Washington.
14 Tunnell, G.A. and Rogers, E.H.I. (1972) *The climate of South Lancashire and North Cheshire.* Climatological Memorandum (69), Meteorological Office, Bracknell.
15 Central Statistical Office (1972) *Annual Abstract of Statistics 1972* HMSO, London.
16 Meteorological Office (1972) Various *Climatological records* Manchester Weather Centre, Manchester.
17 Collier, C.Y. (1970) Fog at Manchester *Weather 25*, 25–9.
18 Meteorological Office (1945–72) *Monthly Weather Reports* HMSO, London.
19 Manchester Weather Centre (1972) Personal communication.
20 General Register Office (1964) *1961 Census, County Reports* HMSO, London.

21 General Register Office (1968) *Sample Census 1966, County Reports* HMSO, London.
22 General Register Office (1972) *1971 Census, Preliminary Report* HMSO, London.
23 Select Committee on Science and Technology (1971) *First Report: Population of the United Kingdom* HMSO, London.
24 SELNEC Transportation Study (SALTS) Group (1970) *1981 and 1984 data summaries by district* Note 68, SALTS, Manchester.
25 Strategic Plan for the North West (1973) *Towards a regional strategy* SPNW (CC) (73) 2, SPNW, Salford.
26 General Register Office (1968) *Sample Census 1966, Economic Activity County Leaflets* HMSO, London.
27 SELNEC Transportation study (SALTS) Group (1968) *Study area characteristics* Technical Working Paper 4, SALTS, Manchester.
28 General Register Office (1968) *Sample Census 1966* Special county print-outs for local authorities with populations of less than 50,000. GRO, London.
29 Joint Working on Structure Plans for Greater Manchester (1973) *Greater Manchester: First review of the study area* Manchester Corporation, Manchester.
30 For example: Second Land Utilization Survey of Britain (1968) *Manchester* E. Stanford, London.
31 Ministry of Agriculture, Fisheries and Food (1972) *Agricultural Returns for Lancashire, Cheshire and Yorkshire* MAFF, London.
32 Lancashire County Council (1969) *Recreational facilities in Lancashire* LCC, Preston.
33 Cheshire County Council (1968) *Recreation in Cheshire* CCC, Chester.
34 SELNEC Transportation Study (SALTS) Group (1972) *Internal working papers and maps* SALTS, Manchester.
35 McLoughlin, J. (1972) *The law relating to pollution* Manchester University Press, Manchester.
36 National Society for Clean Air (1962–73) *Clean Air Yearbook* NSCA, Brighton.
37 *Water Act 1973*.
38 North West Gas Board (1972) Personal communication.
39 Environmental Protection Agency (1972) *Compilation of air pollutant emission factors* Publication AP-042, Government Printing Office, Washington.
40 Department of Trade and Industry (1972) *Digest of United Kingdom Energy Statistics 1972* HMSO, London.
41 Warren Spring Laboratory (1972) *National Survey of air pollution 1961–71, 1* Department of Trade and Industry, HMSO, London.
42 Craxford, S.R., Clifton, M. and Weatherley, M.-L.P.M. (1966) Smoke and sulphur dioxide in Great Britain. *Proc. Int. Clean Air Congr. London (1966)* National Society for Clean Air, Brighton.
43 District Alkali Inspectors (Districts D & E) (1973) Personal communications.

44 *Alkali etc. Works Regulation Act 1906* as extended by the 1966 and 1971 Orders.
45 Drake, K.H.V., Central Electricity Generating Board, North West Region (1973) Personal communication.
46 National Society for Clean Air (1971) *Sulphur dioxide* NSCA, Brighton.
47 *The Motor Vehicles (Construction and Use) (Amendment) (No. 5) Regulations 1972.*
48 *The Motor Vehicles (Construction and Use (Amendment) Regulations 1972* Statutory Instrument 1972 No. 805.
49 Lindsay R. and Thomas, A. (1970) Pollution from road vehicles *Proc. Clean Air Conf. (Southport)* 118–36. National Society for Clean Air, Brighton.
50 Crompton, D.H. and Gilbert, D.G. (1970) Traffic and the environment *Traffic Eng. & Control 12*, 323–6.
51 Reed L.E. and Trott, P.E. (1971) Continuous measurement of carbon monoxide in streets, 1967–9. *Atmos. Environ. 5*, 27–39.
52 Day, J.P. Department of Chemistry, University of Manchester (1973) Personal communication.
53 Pollution Research Unit (1972) *Results of a questionnaire to Public Health Inspectors* Internal paper, PRU, Manchester.
54 Department of the Environment (1973) *Lead and the environment* Circular 6/73, HMSO, London.
55 Lee, J., Department of Botany, University of Manchester (1973) Personal communication.
56 Department of the Environment (1972) *108th Annual Report on Alkali &c. Works 1971* HMSO, London.
57 Derwent, R.G. and Stewart, H.N.M. (1973) Elevated ozone levels in the air of Central London *Nature, Lond. 241*, 342–3.
58 Warren Spring Laboratory (1970) *The Investigation of air pollution: Directory 2: deposit gauge and lead dioxide observations* Department of Trade and Industry, Stevenage.
59 Warren Spring Laboratory (1960–72) *The investigation of air pollution: Deposit gauge and lead dioxide results* Department of Trade and Industry, Stevenage.
60 Rickards, A.L. and Badami, D.V. (1971) Chrysotile asbestos in urban air *Nature, Lond. 234*, 93–4.
61 Rickards, A.L. (1973) The estimation of sub-microgram quantities of chrysotile asbestos by electron microscopy *Anal. Chem. 45*, 809–11.
62 Pollution Research Unit (1972) *Results of a questionnaire to Public Analysts* Internal paper, PRU, Manchester.
63 Department of Trade and Industry (1968–72) *Report of the Government Chemist* HMSO, London.
64 Warren Spring Laboratory (1969) *The investigation of air pollution: Directory 1: daily observations of smoke and sulphur dioxide* Department of Trade and Industry, Stevenage.

65 Warren Spring Laboratory (1960–72) *The investigation of air pollution: National Survey, smoke and sulphur dioxide* Department of Trade and Industry, Stevenage.

66 Warren Spring Laboratory (1973) *National survey of air pollution 1961–71, 2* Department of Trade and Industry, HMSO, London.

67 National Air Pollution Control Administration (1969) *Air quality criteria for particulate matter* Publication AP-049, Government Printing Office, Washington.

68 Brazell, J.H. (1970) Meteorology and the Clean Air Act *Nature, Lond. 226*, 694–6.

69 Wood, C.M. (1973) Visibility and sunshine in Greater Manchester *Clean Air 3 (9)*, 15–24.

70 Wiggett, P.J. (1964) The year-to-year variation of the frequency of fog at London (Heathrow) Airport *Met. Mag. 93*, 305–10.

71 Dinsdale, F.E. (1968) Fog frequencies at inland stations *Met. Mag. 97*, 314–7.

72 Eggleton, A.E.J. and Atkins, D.H. (1972) *Results of the Teeside Investigation* United Kingdom Atomic Energy Authority Report AERE R 6983 HMSO, London.

73 Atkins, J.E. (1968) Changes in visibility characteristics at Manchester/ Ringway Airport *Met. Mag. 97*, 172–4.

74 Lawrence, E.N. (1966) Sunspots—a clue to bad smog? *Weather 21*, 367–70.

75 Lawther, P.J., Waller, R.E. and Henderson, M. (1970) Air pollution and exacerbations of bronchitis. *Thorax, 25*, 525–39.

76 For example: Ayers, S.M. and Buehler, M.R. (1970) Effects of urban air pollution on health. *Clin. Pharmacol. Ther. 11*, 337–71.

77 Ministry of Pensions and National Insurance (1964) *Report on an Enquiry into the Incapacity for Work* HMSO, London.

78 Medical Officer of Health (1969–72) *Annual Reports of Medical Officers of Health* All local authorities in Greater Manchester.

79 Martin, A.E. (1966) Mortality and morbidity statistics in air pollution *Proc. Roy. Soc. Medic. 57*, 969–974.

80 Prescott, T.H.V. (1971) *Aspects of Air Pollution in S.E. Lancashire* M.Sc. Thesis, University of Salford.

81 Royal College of Physicians (1970) *Air Pollution and Human Health* Pitmans Medical, London.

82 Gardner, M.J., Crawford, M.D. and Morris, D.J. (1970) Patterns of mortality in middle and early old age in county boroughs of England and Wales. *Brit. J. prev. soc. Medic. 23*, 133–140.

83 Lowe, C.R. (1970) Clean Air—the health balance sheet. *Proc. Clean Air Conf. Southport* 79–85. National Society for Clean Air, Brighton.

84 Pollution Research Unit (1972) *Results of a questionnaire to Medical Officers of Health.* Internal paper, PRU, Manchester.

85 Moncrief, A.A., Kuomidis, O.P., Clayton, B.F., Patrick, A., Renwick, A.G.C. and Toberts, C.H. (1964) Lead poisoning in children. *Arch. dis. Childn. 39*, 1–13 (and others).

86   Pollution Research Unit (1972) *Results of a questionnaire to Parks and Cemetery Superintendents* Internal paper, PRU, Manchester.

87   Bleasdale, J.K.A. (1952) *Atmospheric pollution and plant growth* Ph.D. Thesis, University of Manchester.

88   Lines, R., Forestry Commission (1971) Personal communication.

89   Webster, C.C. (1967) *Effect of air pollution on plants and soil* Agricultural Research Council, London.

90   Bell, J.N.B. and Clough, W.S. (1973) Depression of yield in rye-grass exposed to sulphur dioxide. *Nature, Lond. 241,* 47–49.

91   Cowling, D.W. and Jones, L.H.P. (1970) A deficiency in soil sulphur supplies for perennial ryegrass in England. *Soil. Sci. 110,* 346–354.

92   Ministry of Agriculture, Fisheries and Food (1971) *Output and utilisation of farm produce in the UK* HMSO, London.

93   Shaw, T.R. (1967) *Interim report on the performance of zinc reference cans as a method of measuring the reducing effects of the atmosphere.* SER/897, Rept. (1/67). Central Electricity Generating Board, London.

94   Fink, F.W., Buttner, F.H. and Boyd, W.K. (1971) *Technical economic evaluation of air pollution corrosion costs on metals in the U.S.* Battelle Memorial Institute, Colombus.

95   Askew, R.R., Cooke, L.M. and Bishop, J.A. (1971) Atmospheric pollution and melanic moths in Manchester and its environs. *J. appl. Ecol. 8,* 247–256.

96   Greater London Council (1970) *The progress and effects of smoke control in London.* Boroughs' Division, GLC Research and Intelligence Unit, London.

97   Department of the Environment (1972) *Report of the working party on refuse disposal* HMSO, London.

98   Local Government Operational Research Unit (1969) *Refuse disposal in north east Cheshire.* Report C51, LGORU, Manchester.

99   Local Government Operational Research Unit (1969) *Refuse disposal in south east Lancashire.* Report C58, LGORU, Manchester.

100 Local Government Operational Research Unit (1971) *Refuse disposal in south Lancashire.* Report C79, LGORU, Manchester.

101 Local Government Operational Research Unit (1971) *Refuse disposal in the Tame Valley area* Report C99, LGORU, Manchester.

102 Ministry of Housing and Local Government (1968) *Public cleansing costing returns* 1965–6, HMSO, London.

103 Pollution Research Unit (1972) *Results of a questionnaire to Cleansing Superintendents* Internal paper, PRU, Manchester.

104 Higginson, A.E. (1965) *The analysis of domestic refuse* Institute of Public Cleansing, London.

105 Lancashire County Council (1972) *Derelict land survey* LCC, Preston.

106 Pollution Research Unit (1973) *Replies to letters to Chief Planning Officers* Internal paper, PRU, Manchester.

107 Joint working on Structure Plans for Greater Manchester (1973) *Derelict land survey* Bolton Corporation, Bolton.

108 Department of the Environment (1971) *Report of the Working Party on Refuse Disposal* Circular 26/71, HMSO, London.

109 Department of the Environment (1972) *Pollution: nuisance or nemesis* HMSO, London.

110 Hanks, T.G. (1967) *Solid waste/disease relationships: a literature survey* Public Health Service Publication 999-VIH-6, Government Printing Office, Washington.

111 Harper, E., Mersey and Weaver River Authority (1973) Personal communication.

112 Local Government Operational Research Unit (1969) *Predicting future quantities of refuse* Report T20, LGORU, Reading.

113 Local Government Operational Research Unit (1969) *Refuse disposal 1981* Report C52, LGORU, Manchester.

114 Local Government Operational Research Unit (1971) *Refuse by rail* Report T31, LGORU, Manchester.

115 Wake, D., Powell Duffryn Pollution Control Ltd., (1972) Personal communication.

116 PFA Marketing Department, Central Electricity Generating Board (1971) Personal communication.

117 Ministry of Housing and Local Government (1970) *Taken for granted* Report of the Working Party on Sewage Disposal, HMSO, London.

118 Pollution Research Unit (1972) *Results of a questionnaire to Sewage Works Managers* Internal paper, PRU, Manchester.

119 Ministry of Housing and Local Government (1954) *Report on the treatment and disposal of sewage sludge* HMSO, London.

120 Department of the Environment (1972) *Out of sight, out of mind* Report of the Working Party on Sludge Disposal in Liverpool Bay, *I* HMSO, London.

121 For example: Ministry of Agriculture, Fisheries and Food (1969) *Farm waste disposal* Short term leaflet No. 67, MAFF, London.

122 For example: Edwards, A.W. and Wibberley, G.P. (1971) *An agricultural land budget for Britain, 1965–2000* Wye College, Wye.

123 Sheard, J., National Coal Board (1971) Personal communication.

124 Department of Trade and Industry (1965–72) *Report of H.M. Inspectors of Mines and Quarries* HMSO, London.

125 Breeze, V.G. (1973) Land reclamation and river pollution problems in the Croal valley caused by chromate manufacture *J. Appl. Ecol. 10,* 513–525.

126 Ministry of Housing and Local Government (1965) *Derelict land* Circular 68/65, HMSO, London.

127 Department of the Environment (1967–72) *North West region—derelict land* DOE, London.

128 Department of the Environment (1973) *Derelict land. New Survey of derelict and despoiled land* Circular 7/73, DOE, London.

129 Cheshire County Council (1972) *Derelict land survey* CCC, Chester.

130 Department of the Environment (1967–72) *Derelict land: summary of returns* DOE, London.

131 *Civic Amenities Act 1967.*
132 Mersey and Weaver River Authority (1972) Personal communication of aggregated river pollution data.
133 Royal Commission on Sewage Disposal (1912) *8th Report* HMSO, London.
134 Department of the Environment (1971) *Report of a river pollution survey of England and Wales 1970–1* HMSO, London.
135 Department of the Environment (1972) *Report of a river pollution survey of England and Wales 1970*, 2 HMSO, London.
136 Abey-Wickrama, I., A'Brook, M.F., Gattoni, F.E.G., and Herridge, C.F. (1969) Mental hospital admission and aircraft noise *The Lancet 7633* 1275–1277.
137 McKennell, A.C. and Hunt, E.A. (1966) *Noise annoyance in Central London* Government Social Survey Unit, HMSO, London.
138 Building Research Station (1968) *London noise survey* Ministry of Public Building and Works, HMSO, London.
139 Association of Public Health Inspectors (1969–72) *Annual Report* APHI, London.
140 Department of Employment and Productivity (1970) *Annual report of H.M Chief Inspector of Factories 1969* HMSO, London.
141 Road Research Laboratory (1970) *A review of road traffic noise* Report LR357, Department of the Environment, Crowthorne.
142 Scholes, W.E. and Sargent, J.W. (1971) Designing against noise from road traffic *Appl. Acoustics 4*, 203–234.
143 Department of Trade and Industry (1973) *Action against aircraft noise* HMSO, London.
144 McLaren, Ward & Partners (1971) *Airport noise at Manchester 1970* Manchester Corporation, Manchester.
145 *Manchester Corporation (General Powers) Act 1971* Part II, Sections 4–11.
146 Cheshire County Council (1973) *Manchester Airport noise: development control policy* CCC, Chester.
147 *Land Compensation Act 1973.*
148 Noise Advisory Council (1971) *Neighbourhood Noise* Department of the Environment, HMSO, London.
149 Department of the Environment (1973) *Planning and Noise* Circular 10/73, HMSO, London.
150 Department of the Environment (1972) *New roads in towns* HMSO, London.
151 Commission on the Third London Airport (1970) *Papers and Proceedings*, 7 HMSO, London.
152 Masefield, P.G. (1973) The air transport scene: present problems—future prospects *Three Banks Review 98*, 1–11.
153 Tulpule, A.H. (1970) *Recent trends in vehicle use in the United States and Britain* Report LR 354, Ministry of Transport, Crowthorne.
154 Lee, N. and Luker, J.A. (1971) An introduction to the economics of pollution *Economics, 9* 19–31.

155 Williams, A.J. (1973) The role of the local planning authority in regard to waste and pollution *J. Planning & Environment Law* (*1973*), 14–22.

156 Burch, W.R., Cheek, N.H. and Taylor, L. (1972) *Social Behaviour, Natural Resources and the Environment* Harper & Row, New York.

157 Lee, N. and Wood, C.M. (1972) Planning and pollution *JRTPI 58*, 153–158.

158 Puffitt, R.G. and Stewart, R.D. (1973) The case for a general purpose environmental inspectorate *Mun. Engng. 150*, 13–17.

159 Organisation for Economic Co-operation and Development (1971) *Models for prediction of air pollution* Environmental Directorate, OECD, Paris.

160 Bowden, K., Green, J.A. and Newsome, D.H. (1971) A mathematical model of the Trent River system. *Proc. Conf. on Trent Research Programme* Institute of Water Pollution Control, London.

161 Aerojet General Corporation (1969) *A systems study of solid waste management in the Fresno area: final report on a solid waste management demonstration* Publication 1959, Public Health Service, Government Printing Office, Washington.

162 Victor, P.A. (1972) *Pollution: economy and environment* George Allen & Unwin, London.

163 For example: Various authors (1973) in *J. Environmental Management 1*, 1–81.

164 Tokyo Metropolitan Government (1971) *Tokyo Fights Pollution* TMG, Tokyo.

165 Greater London Council (1971) *Pollution: a review* GLC, London.

Index